THIS BOOK BELONGS TO
**CONFERENCE RESOURCE LIBRARY**
**2517 North Main St.**
**North Newton, KS 67117**

> "Whoever, therefore, thinks that he understands the divine scriptures or any part of them so that it does not build the double love of God and of our neighbor does not understand it at all."
>
> — St. Augustine

author
**Brandon Hatmaker**
book design
**Peter Schrock**
editorial direction
**Peter Schrock, Caesar Kalinowski, Matt Smay, Hugh Halter**

©2012 Missio Publishing

All scripture NIV unless otherwise noted. Scripture taken from the HOLY BIBLE, NEW INTERNATIONAL VERSION®, NIV® Copyright © 1973, 1978, 1984, 2011 by Biblica, Inc.™ Used by permission. All rights reserved worldwide.

Scripture taken from The Message. Copyright © 1993, 1994, 1995, 1996, 2000, 2001, 2002. Used by permission of NavPress Publishing Group.

All images in this book were taken during a *Serve Austin Sunday* in Austin, Texas. Visit www.austinnewchurch.com for more information.

for more info or to find out about bulk discounts
**tangiblekingdom.com**
**missio.us**

published by Missio Publishing
ISBN 978-0-9830864-2-0
Printed in China

# Barefoot Church *primer*

### an eight-week guide to serving through community

PREPARATION: **Read this first!**     vii

WEEK ONE: **The Journey**     1

WEEK TWO: **Becoming Good News**     25

WEEK THREE: **Mercy**     49

WEEK FOUR: **Justice**     73

WEEK FIVE: **Expose**     97

WEEK SIX: **Experience**     121

WEEK SEVEN: **Engage**     145

WEEK EIGHT: **The Intuitive Life**     169

CLOSING: **What's Next?**     193

I'll never forget the first time I heard someone say that America was a post-Christian society. My mind started reeling and my heart started to thump harder. I even got a little bit angry. That just can't be right, can it? We were founded on the principles of God and country, weren't we?

But the study was showing that more than a million people were leaving the church in America per year. Many of them were claiming a lack of relevance, incongruency with the biblical life of Jesus, or that it simply wasn't adding anything significant to their lives. Many of them were saying things like "There's got to be more to church than this."

More specifically, they were joining the ranks of our critics (holding scripture against us) who say that if the church was being "the Church", we'd be fighting poverty, injustice, and oppression in our world. We would take more seriously God's requirement to love mercy, to seek justice, and our call to a religion that is "pure", fighting for the orphan and the widow.

Most of us agree. But most of us don't know where to start.

Everyone's talking about social action and justice in the world. At the same time, there is a rise of intentionally missional and incarnational communities in the church. For the first time in a long while, a major emphasis of the Western church is on something designed to collectively point people outward and to give them a platform to do so together.

The *Barefoot Church Primer* is designed to be your guide on the journey of "learning to do right." It's designed to put mission back into your small group or faith community. It's designed to help existing churches begin or continue their journey toward being missional, to relearn a posture required to become missionaries to our context, and to equip us to engage culture through engaging the needs of culture. While doing so, we believe you will be changed. You will find community like you've never seen before. And the church will become good news again both to you and to our onlookers.

As we said in the *Tangible Kingdom Primer*, God's ways are natural, but they aren't always easy—especially at first. New ways of life must be formed in us through hours, days, and years of intentional practice. The future of your faith and the incarnational presence of your community are ultimately about letting the Spirit of God re-orient everything about you.

This is why we've called these resources "primers" (which can be defined as a book of elementary principles). While we know a workbook alone won't get the job done, we do think it can provide a good place to start. God's Kingdom doesn't usually unfold in a nice, neat package or linear progression. In fact, he is much more likely to surprise us, to show up in unexpected places and in unique experiences that only he can orchestrate.

Our hope for this book is that it will help you be ready when he does show up. This includes listening and being willing to be changed. It also includes learning to take personal responsibility for your own calling and dealing with those parts of your flesh that keep you from following Jesus as he leads you out into the world.

THE BAREFOOT CHURCH PRIMER
## Not Just About Social Action

While many of you are excited about committing a few weeks to learning how to serve others in need, some come with a fear of it becoming about the act itself, thus missing the heart for a holistic Gospel. Let us eliminate your fear up front—we believe that Jesus calls us to serve the poor, not only to join him in his restoration of God's creation, and certainly not just for the sake of "fixing things."

Along the way we'll learn about how social action can literally change the posture of a church, creating even more opportunities to reach those far from Jesus. We'll see how serving the least not only confronts and exposes our modern view of what it means to be a follower of Christ, we'll also experience it's transforming nature first hand.

One truth always remains—people will always be drawn to good news when they see it in action. It always bears fruit, either in us, or in our onlookers, but most frequently in both.

THE BAREFOOT CHURCH PRIMER
## Where We're Going

Hopefully, you've had a chance to get familiar with the posture and practices of incarnational community by reading *The Tangible Kingdom* and *Barefoot Church* books. Although both books give a broader background of the key concepts, this primer is designed as a stand-alone resource similar to the *TK Primer*. If you are new to faith in Jesus, it will help move you into mission regardless of whether you know a lot of details, history, or theology. If your group is full of those who've been Christians for a long time, each primer will continue to provide a basis for getting beyond the typical "consumer" church experience. For all community leaders, and most participants, we still recommend beginning with *Barefoot Church*. It's a key resource as you begin your journey. But don't let that stop you if you're ready to get going!

As we begin, we'll first provide a quick summary of some key concepts that you will need to understand in order to get everyone in your community on the same page. We'd also like to share a few thoughts that will help you move beyond "just another bible study group experience." Our intent is to provide a new framework for how you can live both naturally and intentionally to make the Gospel of God's Kingdom tangible to you and anyone you love.

We hope that after finishing this eight-week guide, the new habits have become so ingrained in your heart and behavior that the events and projects become intuitive instead of programmed. Most small group guides assume that by completing the assignments you will accomplish the end goal of the small group. Our viewpoint is a little different. We hope that at the end of the eight weeks, you will have successfully begun the journey, not finished it. So, the end is just the beginning! At the end of these next eight weeks, we would love to help you and your community take what you have learned and go to the next level of intentionality; moving even further into forming communities that work to make disciples within a very specific and defined context of people. Keep this in mind as you wrestle through each day and adjust your expectations accordingly.

THE BAREFOOT CHURCH PRIMER
## Basic Concepts

We'll define many of these ideas further as we go through the study, but here are some of the concepts that you can expect to run into:

***Social Action:*** Simple acts of mercy, offering temporary relief, having compassion, and fighting for justice can all be described as social action. Social action typically paints with broad strokes.

***Social Justice:*** While the term social action tends to be more general, social justice typically refers to a more specific effort, with the goal of long-term societal change that brings relief to significant global needs.

***Mercy:*** An attitude of the heart that is disposed toward compassion. Most often translated to mean kindness or goodness. Mercy is often expressed through acts of justice and restoration.

***Justice:*** Often refers to intentionally acting justly or proactively seeking restoration. Justice is an action and a response to the heart of mercy.

***Gospel:*** The news that God has entered the world in Jesus Christ to achieve a salvation that we could not achieve for ourselves. The good news of Jesus is capable of transforming everything about a person, their community, and their world.

***Posture:*** The attitude of the body; the way a person or community expresses itself to others. This is mostly nonverbal.

***Expose:*** To reveal or discover need. Often this comes through an intentional act of research or learning.

***Experience:*** To encounter a new type of need for the first time. This often happens through a more programmed and intentional service project or event.

***Engage:*** To address needs personally or through community. Moving from offering temporary relief to helping eliminate or meet the need as a part of a personal journey.

***The Intuitive Life:*** Our choices, motives, decisions now led by the Holy Spirit. A Spirit-empowered lifestyle guided by a capacity to sense and respond to God's direction.

THE BAREFOOT CHURCH PRIMER
# The Weekly Rhythm

The most difficult part of serving the least is the beginning. Often we take a great idea and get stalled out with the details, easily forgetting a critical step of preparation or a moment of necessary research.

The *Barefoot Church Primer* is designed in such a way to walk you through each phase of the journey one step at a time. First, we will introduce a concept that might be new, giving us an opportunity to absorb and even wrestle with it as we consider what scripture has to say. Each week will then have a practical day of personal action that will be critical to the process.

You might be tempted to get ahead of yourself in planning, but we urge you to maintain the pace provided. Even an old concept needs some fresh consideration. Be sure to prayerfully and purposefully absorb and participate in each step thoroughly. You'll draw and build on each step throughout the eight weeks.

Work hard to be vulnerable and honest with each other during this process. Expect that you might even fight a little along the way. True community doesn't stay shiny and pretty. Sometimes we have to roll around in the mud a bit to find the answers we're looking for. But do us (and yourself) a favor—don't give up on each other and don't give up on "learning" to do right. Trust the Gospel. It really is good news to be "good news."

*"In the same way, let your light shine before others, that they may see your good deeds and glorify your Father in heaven"* [Matthew 5:16].

Although we're following what appears to be a highly structured process, we all know that life doesn't always work like this. Our hope is that the cycle of seven daily practices and reflections will help you begin to understand and incorporate into life the key components to personal and communal renewal.

## Day 1: EXPLORATION

The first day of the weekly rhythm will introduce you to the subject of the week and provide thoughts, stories, and definitions to help you get an understanding of the concepts.

We'll also provide questions and journaling space so that you can wrestle with what this stuff means in your life and in the life of your community. And here's fair warning: we've intentionally written questions that we hope will challenge you. They may even make you uncomfortable sometimes.

We look at it this way—we can make these eight weeks easy and somewhat pointless, or we can make room for the Gospel to get in deep where it can make a difference. The good news is that if you let it, it will change your life. And *that* is what we're after.

## Day 2: MEDITATION

On Day 2, we'll provide you with a scripture or two to soak in for a little while. Read it a couple times and let it do its work in you. Don't forget the questions on the next page.

### Day 3: CHANGE
The Change Day is where we start to get serious. What does this idea mean in your life? How would your life be different if you began to let it be changed by the Gospel? There are questions for journaling on this day as well.

### Day 4: ACTION
So, by now you've begun to let your heart be changed. Now how about your feet? Action Day is about putting it into practice. As we work our way through these eight weeks, we'll give you tasks to do. It's absolutely critical that you follow through with these assignments. The success of your group will depend on it.

### Day 5: COMMUNITY
This day is meant to be a model for how our lives in community are to be increasingly lived out. This is a day when you get together with the other members of your community (those other folks who are putting this stuff into practice along with you) and do something significant together.

In fact, we'll let you in on a secret—this whole process is going to be really difficult to pull off unless you do it with a few friends. Healthy community on mission (with God and with each other) is at the center of all that we're talking about.

### Day 6: CALIBRATION
On Day 6, we'll revisit the theme of the week from a different angle and give you some additional things to think about as you wrestle with the topic of the week and allow God to bring transformation into your life.

### Day 7: RECREATE
The last day of our cycle should include times of rest and reflect a heart that understands Sabbath. This is a reminder to each of us that taking a break is a biblical pattern–one we

like to call ReCreate: we *rest* in Jesus' completed work on our behalf, and out of that rest, we *create* value, beauty, and work. Not to earn God's approval, but creating and working out of the rest we have in Christ.

We intentionally keep Day 7 simple so you can save time for listening. We tend to keep so busy that we couldn't hear from God if he were shouting at us. And he rarely shouts. Try not to rush. Stop for a little while and listen.

**WEEK 1**

# The Journey

# 1.1

THE JOURNEY_*exploration*

# Enjoy the ride

I'll never forget the day my dad drove up. It was 1984 and I was standing outside when he rounded the corner in a "new to us" 1972 Winnebago Brave. ■ I want you to picture this thing for a moment. It was white with brown and orange stripes. It had big plaid Captain's Chairs that swiveled 180-degrees, a sweet kitchenette, and an 8-track player that, I kid you not, came with a fully equipped selection of Willie Nelson, The Gatlin Brothers, and the Oak Ridge Boys Gospel Hits. ■ It…was…awesome! For us kids, it completely changed the way we felt about family vacations. It was no longer just about where we were going. It quickly became about the journey to get there. We learned to enjoy the ride.

Learning to serve is necessary for anyone seeking to be an apprentice of Jesus. With this in mind, our hope is that you can embrace the next eight weeks as part of your journey in becoming more like Christ. And we hope you'll give yourself permission to celebrate the victories along the way. ■ We don't have to look far into the life of Jesus to realize that it was often on his *journey* that he accomplished so much. They were "along the way" moments, the times that most of us would consider an interruption or waste of time.

■ For Jesus, it's where the unexpected became the expected:

✚ Jesus was simply *"passing by"* when the first disciples saw him and decided to follow [John 1].
✚ Jesus was on a *journey* to Jerusalem for the Passover feast when he stopped for a wedding in Cana and turned water into wine [John 2].
✚ Jesus was *on his way* to Galilee, *passing through* Samaria, when he spoke with the woman at the well [John 4].
✚ Jesus was once again *on his way* to Jerusalem when he healed the man at the sheep gate pool just outside the city gates [John 5].
✚ Jesus was *crossing to the far shore* of the Sea of Galilee when a large crowd began to follow him and he miraculously fed the five thousand [John 6].
✚ It was *"as Jesus went along"* that he saw a man who was "blind from birth," and during this moment of margin he put mud on the man's eyes and gave him sight [John 9].
✚ Jesus was simply walking along Solomon's Porch when the Jews began to question him about being the Christ [John 10].

There's a lot to learn on our journey. And as a part of a community of faith seeking to be Good News to a world in need of some good news, I beg you not to miss it. What we sometimes forget is that our individual journey will impact our collective experience. We can trust that God is up to something great for both.

## 1.1 NOTES

◯ Think through a few of the unexpected things you've experienced "along the way" on your journey that turned out to be significant and life-shaping. List them below.

◯ What do you think God was teaching you through those things?

◯ Have you ever missed an opportunity to help someone in need because you were too busy or not paying attention "along the way?" How could you have responded differently?

◯ Learning to serve often starts with simple steps of awareness. What are some things you can do to be more aware of opportunities in your day? What could you stop doing to make space?

# 1.2

**Scripture reminds us that** love expresses itself in a growing appreciation for God, an increasingly merciful heart, and compassionate action for others. This is where the idea of journey becomes a reality. The book of James challenges us to consider how we become "doers" of the Word, not just "learners" of the Word, ultimately calling it pure religion. In 1 Corinthians 13, Paul teaches boldly about the significance of love.

> *If I speak in the tongues of men or of angels, but do not have love, I am only a resounding gong or a clanging cymbal. If I have the gift of prophecy and can fathom all mysteries and all knowledge, and if I have a faith that can move mountains, but do not have love, I am nothing. If I give all I possess to the poor and give over my body to hardship that I may boast, but do not have love, I gain nothing.* ■ *Love is patient, love is kind. It does not envy, it does not boast, it is not proud. It does not dishonor others, it is not self-seeking, it is not easily angered, it keeps no record of wrongs. Love does not delight in evil but rejoices with the truth. It always protects, always trusts, always hopes, always perseveres.* ■ *Love never fails. But where there are prophecies, they will cease; where there are tongues, they will be stilled; where there is knowledge, it will pass away. For we know in part and we prophesy in part, but when completeness comes, what is in part disappears. When I was a child, I talked like a child, I thought like a child, I reasoned like a child. When I became a man, I put the ways of childhood behind me. For now we see only a reflection as in a mirror; then we shall see face to face. Now I know in part; then I shall know fully, even as I am fully known.* ■ *And now these three remain: faith, hope and love. But the greatest of these is love.* [1 Corinthians 13:1-13]

The greatest of these is love—because God is love. But true love takes action. God acts and reveals his love through the sacrifice of his son [John 15:9-15, John 3:16]. Love that feels sympathy without acting compassionately falls desperately short of Jesus' vision for his disciples. There's a huge difference between feeling bad for someone and doing something about it. *But often we don't know where to start.*

THE JOURNEY_*meditation*

# Pray for wisdom

The book of James says if we lack wisdom, we should pray for it: "If any of you lacks wisdom, you should ask God, who gives generously to all without finding fault, and it will be given to you." [James 1:5]

James writes that wisdom applied teaches us:
- That we should live, not just learn, the Bible [James 1:22].
- That pure religion cares for the orphan and widow [James 1:27].
- That loving our neighbor is the "royal law" [James 2:8].
- That mercy triumphs over judgment [James 2:13].
- That faith without deeds is worthless [James 2:16,20].
- That knowledge should result in humble deeds [James 3:13].
- That wisdom from heaven is full of mercy [James 3:15-17].
- That failing to do "good" is sin [James 4:17].
- That in our neglect we become the oppressors [James 5:1-6].

## 1.2 NOTES

◉ Paul wrote to the church at Corinth that love "always protects, always trusts, always hopes, and always perseveres." Take a moment to ponder these truths. Why do you think Paul felt it necessary to remind this young church about these things?

◉ As a faith community, in what ways do you feel WE are called to protect? Trust? Hope? And persevere? How about as it relates to those outside the church? How about to those in need?

◉ Throughout all of scripture, we see love ultimately expressing itself as action. James says that faith without works is literally worthless. As you consider how love is actively being and should be lived out in your life, how often is your faith expressing itself in loving action?

◉ What challenges get in the way of you "living love" more regularly? How could these challenges be overcome?

## 1.3

# A new way of thinking

Paul describes the problem: *For I have the desire to do what is good, but I cannot carry it out. For I do not do the good I want to do* [Romans 7:18b-20].

Why is this? Here's his answer: *For the flesh desires what is contrary to the Spirit, and the Spirit what is contrary to the flesh. They are in conflict with each other.* [Galatians 5:17]

Many of us have faced the same struggle. When will I actually want to serve those in need? When will I come to the place where I'm willing to give up my stuff for the sake of others? The good news is that it's all a part of the journey–a journey that is led by the Spirit. A few crucial shifts in our belief help our hearts turn the corner:

+ We need to be honest with ourselves and God about our own spiritual poverty and need. We are lost without him!

+ We need to believe that God served us in the ultimate way through the life, death and resurrection of his son Jesus.

+ We need to see that everything we have received along the journey is ultimately for the serving of others for God's glory. (Talent, education, relationships, resources etc.)

+ We need to consider and even confess our self-focused lives and neglect of others needs.

+ We need to believe that we are just as loved and accepted by God when we serve others as when we don't.

+ We need to start somewhere, trusting God to do the work.

I received an email the other day from one of the founding members of our church. His story is simple—he's an extremely successful businessman who's done just about everything in life. Through serving the "least" he has been radically changed by God…

## THE JOURNEY_change

Brandon,

Just wanted to put words to what's been going on in my life over the last few years and share it with you. You know that each time we do the homeless grill-out downtown that my post is at the front of the line handing out the tickets. I love it because I get to talk to everyone we serve.

In case you didn't know, they call me "Ticket Man."

They have called me that for a few years now. A few years of my own metamorphosis from "dude too busy to notice suffering" or "dude too quick to judge who deserves help" to "ticket-man."

I hand out tickets so that we make sure we have enough hamburgers for everyone in line. I am no longer "dude who flies first-class to Sydney" or "dude having a drink at the top of the JW Marriott in Hong Kong," just "Ticket Man."

Something happens when you serve. Something you cannot control. You start with all sorts of obstacles, fear, incompetence and even a desire to avoid the hopelessness that occurs when you realize that you do not have the power within you to fix people.

Something changes and you stop seeing people and you see a person. Maybe even for a fleeting second you see a person through his eyes. And you see their heart and they see yours. And you see them see your heart and that is when you get it. Serving was never about them.

Serving is about getting gripped in the heart by God. And he touches your heart through the ones you serve. I am not who I was. And it has nothing to do with anything I did. It is the heart connection to individuals as you serve with no agenda other than telling them, "I see you, you are a person and I accept you for who you are in this moment."

I am Ticket Man and serving has been transformational for me.

                                                             Thanks, Alex

## 1.3 NOTES

◉ Think through the shifts in thinking about heart change (page 10). Which ones are the most difficult for you to truly grab hold of? How would your life change if these truths began to take root deep in your beliefs about you, God, and serving others?

◉ How do you feel about the "tension" between what you think you should be doing for others, and what you actually do? How does this affect your actions?

◆ How does the belief that God loves you the same whether you serve others or not change your motivation to serve?

◆ Write down a few things you could easily do yet have neglected doing? What kept you from doing them in the first place?

## 1.4

## Our best offering

The *Barefoot Church* book is based around the story where an entire church was challenged to leave their shoes on the altar while taking communion. The shoes were to be given to the homeless in the community. It was a beautiful reminder that the altar is not just a place to receive, but also a place to lock arms with Jesus and give.

*It feels like just yesterday that I turned around to look up the stairs and saw an entire church being sent out into a city ...barefoot. It was clear what Jesus was saying: "This is how I want my church to look, a place where love and self-sacrifice is hardwired into the DNA of my people, of solidarity with the poor, and true community rallied around my Gospel. I want a Church where the altar is not only a place to take communion, but also a place to leave your shoes. I want a barefoot church.* [from *Barefoot Church: Serving the Least in a Consumer Culture*]

## THE JOURNEY_action

No one planned on giving away the shoes they had on that day. It was quite unexpected. That was the best part. It was a cold day and it was Easter Sunday. Translation: We all had on our best (and mostly new) shoes. They were the best we had to offer, and it was hard to give them away. ■ The *Barefoot Church Primer* is designed to help us engage need together as a part of community. The "whole" truly becomes "greater than the sum of its parts." However, as a part of the "whole," and as a part of your first action day, we want you to do three simple things individually:

### [1]  Look for Need // Pray for it

Pray right now that God would literally open your eyes to simple needs around you today. Work hard to keep it at the front of your mind all day.

### [2]  Commit to Need // Whatever it is

Here's what will happen—if you're prayerfully looking, you will see need today. It may be as simple as helping someone with a flat tire or handing a bottled-water to a homeless man on the corner. The key is listening to the Spirit and deciding in advance to do whatever it is. Make the commitment now to say "yes."

### [3]  Meet the Need // Take action

When you see the need, do whatever you can to help. If you can't do it, don't stress about it (this is key and we'll wrestle with that tension later). Focus today on what you CAN do, not what you can't.

Take note of what happened as you practiced discovering need, committing to it, and taking action. Be prepared to share tomorrow when your group gets together whether you could do anything about it or not.

## 1.5

# Getting together for the first time

As you meet for the first time as a community, here are some things to do to kick it off:

Spend a little extra time just "hanging out" at the beginning of this time. Enjoy some food together before you start.

If you haven't already, exchange contact information to make it easier for your community to stay connected.

Do something fun.

**Suggested questions for group discussion:**
On the first day (1.1), we talked about the idea of "journey." Share with the group some of the unexpected experiences you've had "along the way."

On day two (1.2), we took a biblical look at how love manifests itself into action. Share with the group your answers to the question, "What challenges get in the way of you living 'love' more regularly?"

On day three (1.3), we discussed the idea of transformation. Share with the group your thoughts on the questions, "How do you feel about the 'tension' between what you think you should be doing for others, and what you actually do? How does this affect your actions?"

On day four (1.4), we were challenged to simply pray, look for, and meet a simple need that came up through the day. Take a moment to share with the group about your day.

What are you learning about yourself and creating "margin" for mission? Have you ever felt the tension or pressure of *arrival* over *journey*? How does the idea of giving each other permission or margin to live life "as you go" impact that tension? Why?

**NEXT STEPS:** Take a moment to discuss among your group any immediate needs you might know of in your community, workplaces, or schools. It might be a single mom in need, someone sick, or a family you know going through some tough times. The goal is to just begin increasing awareness of needs that might exist right under your noses. Pray for them. (This will also help you get a jump on your Action day for next week.)

## 1.6

## Serving the least

**There are more than 2200 verses** in the Bible that talk about serving the least. In fact, one of God's greatest indictments of the nation of Israel was often more about what they'd neglected to do in regards to the poor than anything else. The impact of neglect is greater than we know. At one point in Isaiah chapter 1, God says that, because of their neglect, their worship has literally become meaningless to him.

The biblical solution to their problem?

*Learn to do right; seek justice. Defend the oppressed. Take up the cause of the fatherless; plead the case of the widow* [Isaiah 1:17]. *Let us discern for ourselves what is right; let us learn together what is good* [Job 34:4]. *But go and learn what this means: 'I desire mercy, not sacrifice'* [Matthew 9:13].

God instructs us to learn to do right. Learning is the foundation of our journey. The key is in the willingness to learn. So often we get bogged down with failing to do right that we forget to take the time and put in the effort to learn what it looks like. Later, Isaiah points out that it's not only that they didn't defend the orphan or widow, it's that they didn't even see their need.

*Side Note:* A key element of "learning to do right" is found in learning to see the need around us. While we'll spend the next few weeks creating a biblical framework for serving, in week five we'll begin to peel the layers back on exposing, experiencing, and engaging need.

## Excerpt from Barefoot Church:

*Recently, my wife Jen and I were having an all-too-familiar conversation with a young couple that had given up on church. Not a specific church, THE church. While both of them had attended since birth, and had even served a few years in ministry, they had become jaded and had joined the ranks of those claiming that, "Church—as we see it—is not for us."*

*When given a chance to share specifics on the thing that "what's-his-name" had said or what "so-and-so" had done, the young wife exploded passionately with a single-themed indictment: "The church needs to care more about the poor! They need to fight injustice! They need to help the orphan and widow in their distress! They need to do what they say they're about!"*

*Silence.*

*Surprising even herself, and with a slightly stunned look on her face, she calmly said as a tear rolled down her cheek, "Here's the problem: I don't do it either. I don't know how. I don't even know where to start."*

*That was a big moment for me. It's easy to cast stones. It's easy to point out the problems in the existing church. And it's just as easy to pretend we're not a part of the problem. But this was a refreshingly honest confession of ownership that I've come to find so many believers identifying with. They want to do something of more significance, but they don't event know where to start.*

## 1.6 NOTES

◎ Have you ever learned to do something related to your faith that didn't come naturally to you? What was it? Why was it so hard to do? What might God be wanting you to learn now?

◎ Can you identify with the young woman in the story who said, *"The church needs to care more about the poor! They need to fight injustice! They need to help the orphan and widow in their distress! They need to do what they say they're about!"* How does this identification prompt your heart?

◆ As you look at the rhythm of your life, do you think you could be accused of "neglecting the poor" as Israel was? Whatever your answer, how do you think God feels about this? How do you feel?

◆ Take a moment and write a personal prayer response to God responding to all of this. Stay away from promises. Focus on confession. Pray for wisdom.

# 1.7

**Throughout this study, we'll wrap up each week with a challenge to remain intentionally restful.** This day should help you recalibrate to the biblical pattern of Sabbath. If today is not a day you can fully set aside to rest, look for an alternative later in the week.

Either way, include the ideas and thoughts from Day 7 into your regular weekly day of rest. We find it helpful to think of this rhythm as ReCreate: we *rest* in Jesus and out of that rest we *create* value, beauty, work and service to others.

*Thus the heavens and the earth were completed in all their vast array. By the seventh day God had finished the work he had been doing; so on the seventh day he rested from all his work. Then God blessed the seventh day and made it holy, because on it he rested from all the work of creating that he had done* [Genesis 2:1-3].

After God finished creating the earth, animals, and humans, he rested. It was as if he said, "It is finished!" Right before Jesus died on the cross for our sins he cried out to the Father, "It is finished!" Now we can truly live all of life—even the parts where we work and serve others—not to earn God's approval, but within this reality of resting in the completed work of Christ on our behalf. *"It is finished!"*

The Bible teaches us that resting is not about inactivity. It is a condition of the heart. If you work in an office most days, perhaps you can find true *soul rest* in gardening or painting a picture or composing a song. If your daily life is hectic and fast paced then resting is all about slowing down and making space to be with and listen to God. As humans, we were not created to live our lives at full speed without regular rhythms of rest thrown in to reconnect us to God and his plans for our life.

*Remember the Sabbath day by keeping it holy. Six days you shall labor and do all your work, but the seventh day is a sabbath to the LORD your God* [Exodus 20:8-9].

*There remains, then, a Sabbath-rest for the people of God; for anyone who enters God's rest also rests from their works, just as God did from his. Let us, therefore, make every effort to enter that rest...* [Hebrews 4:9-11].

THE JOURNEY_reCreate

**Consider this:** In what ways in the past have you served others out of a sense of duty or guilt? What would it be like to serve out of a truly rested and secure heart that is focused on God's unconditional love for you, letting him show others his love along the journey of your life?

**WEEK 2**

# Becoming Good News

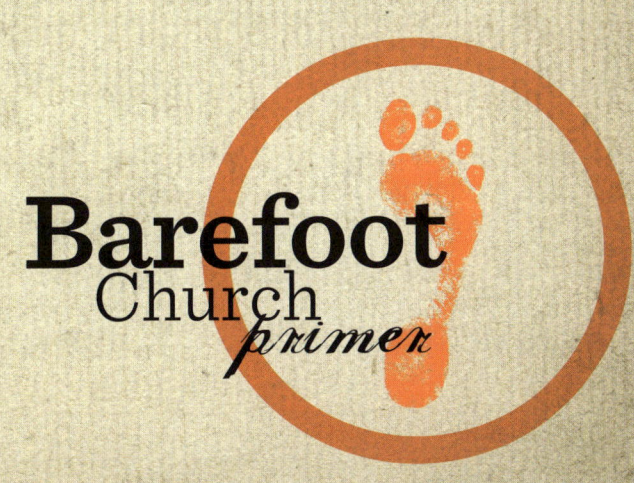

# 2.1

**I was leaving a downtown meeting** last summer when I got a flat tire in the middle of rush hour. It was the middle of August and the temperature was easily into the triple digits.

Perfect.

After unloading my entire trunk, I had just managed to get out the spare and locate the jack when a man carrying a bible approached me. I'll never forget looking over my shoulder at him with sweat dripping in my eyes when he asked if I needed help.

"Sure." I replied. "Can you loosen the lug nuts while I get the jack?"

"Not with your tire, help with your life." He continued, "Let me ask you a question, if you were hit by a car right now and died, do you know where you'd go?"

Are you serious? Listen, I'm thankful this guy was so passionate about sharing his faith. But, I couldn't help but think how ineffective that would have been had I not been a believer. In fact, I could just imagine the fuel for fodder that would be for a skeptic of the church.

This guy truly believed in the message he wanted to share. He knew it was more important than a fixed flat. He had Good News. But at the time, he wasn't good news to me. I'd just prefer he helped me with my flat.

# Knowing and Being

Jesus taught a new way, with a new hope, making all things new. He didn't just have good news, he literally became good news to a lost and dying world. He invites us to do the same. ■ In order for us to do this, it is important that we gain an accurate understanding of the Gospel as "good news". It may require that we do some rebuilding. Many of us have an understanding of the Gospel as proclamation or spoken evangelism, but often our idea ends there. ■ It is important that we have a full, robust picture of the Gospel, and that it is becoming increasingly rooted in all areas of our lives. *So how is the Gospel good news?* ■ The Gospel is particularly good news regarding our sin problem. This is certainly something we cannot handle on our own. God himself has come to rescue and renew his creation through Jesus. ■ Why does creation (including us) need rescuing? It's because of sin. ■ All rebellion against God and his ways is sin. It is living life my own way, for me, instead of living life God's ways, for him. We have all sinned and need the Gospel—we desperately need Jesus to rescue us from the penalty and effects of sin, which the Bible teaches is ultimate and eternal separation from God. When we, by faith, put our trust in Jesus' life, death, and resurrection, the power of the Gospel saves and restores our lives. ■ Eventually the whole world will be renewed to the way God originally created it. Rebellion, death, decay, injustice, and suffering will all be removed. When everything is restored, God will be seen by all for who he truly is—he will be glorified.

## 2.1 NOTES

◉ Have you looked at sin in your life through the lens of rebellion against God and his ways? In what areas of your life are you still living according to *your* ways?

◉ What areas of your life is God still wanting to bring restoration to? Mentally? Emotionally? Physically?

◉ Has anyone ever tried to "share faith" with you before they took the time to hear your story or ask if you had the time to talk? What can you learn from their "strategy?"

◉ Think of someone you know who is not yet a believer. How might you begin to better understand what the "good news" could look and sound like, specifically, in this person's life? List at least 3 ways.

◉ In light of your thoughts to the last question, how could you connect the Gospel good news of Jesus directly to this person's life and needs?

◉ Have you struggled with the tension between "sharing" faith and "doing" good works? What is your greatest concern? Where does that concern come from?

## 2.2

## Head, Heart, and Hands

Biblically, we should consider three ways that the Gospel works in our lives:

**DOCTRINE**
*The Gospel saves. It is the announcement that Jesus died on the cross for our sins and rose from the dead, thus conquering death and sin. This is the announcement of a historical event that has eternal impact.*

**PERSONAL**
*The Gospel transforms. The Gospel rewrites our personal story as it changes our hearts, minds, and priorities.*

**SOCIAL**
*The Gospel renews. While it is not contingent upon us, the Gospel invites us into the making of "all things new," giving hope and restoring what was broken.*

**God has given us both the *message* of reconciliation and the *ministry* of reconciliation.**

*Therefore, if anyone is in Christ, he is a new creation; the old has gone, the new has come! All this is from God, who reconciled us to himself through Christ and gave us the **ministry** of reconciliation: that God was reconciling the world to himself in Christ, not counting men's sins against them. And he has committed to us the **message** of reconciliation* [2 Corinthians 5:17-19].

*In the same way, let your light shine before others, that they may see your good deeds and glorify your Father in heaven* [Matthew 5:16].

Why is this so important? Jesus understood that our actions give credibility to our words. He also knew that not everyone would believe with words alone, that for some the greatest evidence would be our words lived out.

*Believe me when I say that I am in the Father and the Father is in me; or at least **believe on the evidence of the works** themselves* [John 14:11].

This requires us to not only speak about Jesus. It challenges us to live out his ways. The two must go together. Proclamation and incarnation are inseparably linked. It may be simpler to live as if our actions and words function independently of each another, but one thing's for certain—our observers never separate the two.

## 2.2 NOTES

*If the work of the Gospel seems to stop at our own personal conversion, we need to take a hard look at how we define it. For those of us who have grown up with a one-dimensional view of the Gospel, this may require a complete shift in thinking. Yet our hope should always be to champion the Gospel and expand the Kingdom, not limit it. This reality challenges us to not only ponder what we're doing, but even more so, what more could be done.*

◉ How might the way you live your faith change if you viewed the Gospel as being doctrinal, personal, and social?

Considering the three "Perspectives of the Gospel," place an "X" on the line to evaluate where you are in each area.

◉ **Doctrinal Understanding**

*Not so hot* — *Pretty good*

*Doctrinal understanding* starts with each of us personally grasping the Gospel's implication in our lives. We must settled the issue of salvation and understand fully our redemption in Christ and his call to mission.

## ⊙ Personal Transformation

*Not so hot*                                                                 *Pretty good*

*Personal transformation* is our story rewritten. It means a change in our hearts and mind. True transformation impacts every facet of your life, addressing issues of consumerism, materialism, and individualism. This requires a submission to the Spirit and the literal presentation of ourselves as a living sacrifice to the ways of Jesus.

## ⊙ Social Restoration

*Not so hot*                                                                 *Pretty good*

*Social restoration* begins and ends with love of mercy and seeking of justice. We are called to be agents of reconciliation and hope for the broken, oppressed, marginalized, abandoned, and helpless. It recognizes that by our silence, we become the oppressors.

## 2.3

Who is going to harm you if you are eager to do good? ■ But even if you should suffer for what is right, you are blessed. "Do not fear their threats; do not be frightened." ■ But in your hearts revere Christ as Lord. Always be prepared to give an answer to everyone who asks you to give the reason for the hope that you have. But do this with gentleness and respect, ■ keeping a clear conscience, so that those who speak maliciously against your good behavior in Christ may be ashamed of their slander. ■ It is better, if it is God's will, to suffer for doing good than for doing evil. ■ For Christ also suffered once for sins, the righteous for the unrighteous, to bring you to God. [1 Peter 3:13-18]

In verse 14, Peter reminds us that we should "always be prepared" to give an answer for the hope that we have. This verse makes one major assumption:

## It assumes that someone is actually asking.

He is clearly challenging us to live a life in such a way that others will take notice. This is a key part of the Gospel. People saw the love of Jesus, they recognized his humility, his concern, his compassion, and the hope that he offered. They were drawn to him, and they were always asking him questions.

There's another tension brought up in this passage: Those who do good will often suffer. Peter is reminding us that it's not always easy and it is often the religious who throw stones. He tells us that when we suffer for doing good, we are blessed. He challenges us not to fear but to set our hearts on the things of Christ.

Many believers learning to engage need go through a season of doubt or even persecution. Often they wonder if, through their service, they are somehow compromising the Gospel. Peter reminds us that there will always be others who won't view serving the same as you. But, despite this, he encourages us to stay the course.

## 2.3 NOTES

◉ Peter challenges us to "be prepared to give an answer" for the hope we profess. Do you think this is more about defending our faith, proclaiming our faith, or both? Explain your answer.

◉ Have you ever shied away from sharing your faith in a conversation? (Most of us have!) Why do you think this happens?

◆ How prepared do you feel to verbally share the Gospel in natural, meaningful ways with people? What could you begin to do to learn and be better prepared? Ask God to show you.

◆ Has anyone ever asked you about your faith without you bringing it up? Why do you think that is? What things could you do to increase the possibility or frequency of that happening?

◆ Have you ever had to "suffer" for doing good? What happened? What did you learn?

## 2.4

> Learn to do right;
> Seek justice.
> Defend the oppressed.
> —Isaiah 1:17

The book of Isaiah teaches that our task is *to learn to do what is right*. This points out a big sticking point for many believers—we want to do something, but often don't even know where to start.

This is also good news to us. It's no surprise to God that we don't know what we're doing. He gives us space to be learners. Maybe the test is in our *willingness* to try.

Today we're going to take a practical first step. It won't require you to go anywhere or talk to anyone. But the success of everything we do in the coming weeks will hinge upon how seriously you take today's exercises. Your involvement will impact both you and your group. (Be prepared to share your notes with your community tomorrow. We will be making a collective list of opportunities to serve).

Take a moment to think about people you already know who are in need. This might be a person at work, a family down the street, or someone you've heard about. Make a list below describing their need. Try to come up with at least three names:

**Name**                **Need**

BECOMING GOOD NEWS_*action*

Go online and search out any non-profits, "cause" groups, or benefit organizations in your community. Start with those you know or who are closest to where you live. List those organizations below. Include phone numbers and web addresses:

**Name**               **Contact**               **Website**

Consider other opportunities to serve that might not be related to a non-profit or established organization but would be something your group could do together. List them below.

# 2.5

## Let's get practical

Before we get started with our group discussion today, we're going to do some planning for next week's gathering where we will be making supply kits for the homeless in your city. Take a moment to assign responsibilities for the following items (bring enough for everyone in your group to make 5 kits.) Be creative. For example, dentists and hotels will often donate some of the items on the list.

Amount of each item we need: _____

| Items | Who's Bringing Them |
|---|---|
| Quart-sized Ziploc bags | _____ |
| Bar of Soap | _____ |
| Toothbrush | _____ |
| Comb | _____ |
| Travel-sized toothpaste | _____ |
| Travel-sized shampoo | _____ |
| Travel-sized deodorant | _____ |
| Pair of socks | _____ |
| Bottle of water | _____ |
| Other | _____ |
| *Note cards and markers | _____ |

*The note cards and makers are optional. You can invite the kids from the group to make cards with blessings, words of encouragement, or even scriptures on each. This can be a great way to get the kids involved. Be sure to give them suggestions on what's appropriate to write.

**If there are no homeless people** in your community, consider making the kits and taking a trip to an urban destination to pass them out. Or come up with an alternate idea. For example, you could bring ingredients to make meals together for a needy family or one who just had a baby. Collect items for a food drive. Make "care packages" for teachers at the local school. Assemble kits of useful items for the elderly that you could deliver to the local nursing home. The key is to 1) be creative, 2) serve someone from outside of your faith community, 3) involve everyone in your group, and 4) make sure no one feels like they owe you for what you've done.

**Suggested questions for group discussion:**
On the first day (2.1), we talked a little about how a holistic Gospel includes both words and action. Share with the group your answers to the questions: Have you struggled with the tension between "sharing" faith and "doing" good works? What is your greatest concern? Where does that concern come from?

On day two (2.2), we took a look at how "doing good" often comes with a form of suffering. What fear do you have regarding serving the poor? Share your examples.

On day four (2.4), we were challenged to make a list of non-profit organizations in our community. Take a moment to review everyone's list and make a "top five" list of potential organizations that your group could partner with.

**PRAY FOR THOSE IN NEED:** Last week we discussed those in your community with needs. This week's day of action we each made a list of those people. As you close your time today, take a moment to pray for each of them by name. Ask God to help them and to show whether or not your group should take action to help them. You can't help everyone, but you can at least pray for them.

## 2.6

Most people are looking for a reason to believe. They are drawn to whatever is good news. ■ Tim Keller has written that *"The Gospel ... is not just about individual happiness and fulfillment. It is not just a wonderful plan for 'my life' but a wonderful plan for the world. It is about the coming of God's kingdom to renew everything. Gospel-centered churches do not only urge individuals to be converted, but also to seek peace and justice in our cities and in our world."*

But do we really care?

BECOMING GOOD NEWS_*calibration*

"I was in New Orleans on a mission trip one time with a group of missionaries set on saving the city. Everyone was on Bourbon Street handing out evangelism tracts when I sat down with a homeless man and asked him, 'What do you think about all these Christians out here 'tract bombing' you guys?'"

He replied, "You know, I'm sure these guys care about what they believe and what they're doing. I'm just not sure they care about us." - *Matthew Hansen, Director of Restore Communities*

## 2.6 NOTES

◉ How much has Christianity, and your own personal faith, been focused on the "afterlife" compared to what God is wanting to do in the world around you, today, right now?

◉ What are some good examples of faith in action you have seen or experienced?

◉ What would it look like to seek peace and justice in your city or community? Give a few examples:

◗ How does Matthew's experience in New Orleans make you feel? Can you relate? What thoughts come to mind about his conversation with the homeless man?

◗ If we were to constantly speak a message that was not consistent with our actions, how would that impact our credibility? How would the church be viewed?

**2.7**

For it is by grace you have been saved, through faith—and this not from yourselves, it is the gift of God—not by works, so that no one can boast. For we are God's workmanship, created in Christ Jesus to do good works, which God prepared in advance for us to do. [Ephesians 2:8-10]

BECOMING GOOD NEWS_reCreate

**Consider this:** God's grace leads to faith that leads to salvation that leads to good works. In his grace, God reached out and found you, saved you and has prepared specific works for you to do in his Kingdom. But notice in Ephesians 2 that it is all his initiation—his work—so we can work. Ultimately it is God who saves, renews and restores all things. The pressure is off! We can rest in his perfect plan and timing for our lives and the lives of others.

WEEK 3

# Mercy

## 3.1

# The heart of mercy

*Mercy* and *justice* are themes found throughout scripture, which describes the reasons and methods for engaging need. Mercy is most often translated to mean kindness, goodness, or compassion—it's the heart and motivation behind the action. The word comes from a Hebrew word that literally means to "bow the neck in courtesy; to be kind." In order to seek justice, we must first understand mercy.

> Mercy is a command of God, yet it cannot simply be a response to a demand. It must arise out of hearts made generous and gracious by an understanding and experience of God's mercy. It is the hearts of the [people] that must be melted until they ask, "Where [or who] is my neighbor?"
>
> - Tim Keller

Simply put, mercy offers immediate and compassionate treatment of those in distress. It's the first step to engaging need and acts as a filter for our motivation. Thus, developing a heart of mercy is the natural next step of our journey. ■ Mercy is an attitude of the heart that is disposed toward compassion. In the economy of the Kingdom, mercy has a reciprocal effect—as we grow in mercy, and respond to need, we also become the recipients of mercy. One who would receive mercy must show mercy. ■ The motivations that Jesus emphasized the most in his teachings, and that were reflected in his life, were love and mercy. Although God is just, his mercy is abundant. Together they give a true picture of his love. Through them, we see a true image of God, which we hope to mirror.

> *He has shown you, O mortal, what is good. And what does the LORD require of you? To act justly and to love mercy and to walk humbly with your God. [Micah 6:8]*

## 3.1 NOTES

⊙ The Bible challenges us to "love" mercy and seems to initially focus more on the heart or attitude of mercy rather than the action. How does this line up with your idea of mercy?

⊙ What does a lack of love of mercy show about our understanding of God's mercy toward us?

◉ In what ways has God shown you mercy in your life? In little ways? In big ways?

◉ Scripture urges us, in view of God's mercies, to "present ourselves as a living sacrifice" [Rom 12:1-2]. How does a deeper understanding of God's mercies in your life increase your love of mercy?

## 3.2

***In Jesus' teaching,*** we see the need for a bigger understanding of mercy. He's literally saying that, without it, we miss the forest for the trees. *Woe to you, teachers of the law and Pharisees, you hypocrites! You give a tenth of your spices—mint, dill and cumin. But you have neglected the more important matters of the law—justice, mercy and faithfulness. You should have practiced the latter, without neglecting the former. You blind guides! You strain out a gnat but swallow a camel.* [Matthew 23:23-24] ■ *"I desire mercy, not sacrifice." For I have not come to call the righteous, but sinners.* [Matthew 9:13] ■ *Come, let us return to the LORD. He has torn us to pieces but he will heal us; he has injured us but he will bind up our*

MERCY_*meditation*

*wounds. After two days he will revive us; on the third day he will restore us, that we may live in his presence. Let us acknowledge the LORD, let us press on to acknowledge him. As surely as the sun rises, he will appear; he will come to us like the winter rains, like the spring rains that water the earth. What can I do with you, Ephraim? What can I do with you, Judah? Your love is like the morning mist, like the early dew that disappears. Therefore I cut you in pieces with my prophets, I killed you with the words of my mouth—then my judgments go forth like the sun. For I desire mercy, not sacrifice, and acknowledgment of God rather than burnt offerings.* [Hosea 6:1-6]

## 3.2 NOTES

⊙ What do you think it means to value or desire mercy above sacrifice? Why do you think this reflects the true heart of God?

⊙ The Old Testament prophets often instructed Israel to "fix" their situation through their attitude and heart of service to those in needs. Why do you think that was such a common tactic? What does it tell you about the nation of Israel?

◐ What did the idea of *mercy* mean to them?

◐ What aspects of mercy are most alive to you in this point in your spiritual pilgrimage?

# A shift in thinking

Through the way he lived, Jesus often challenged us, pointing out the discrepancy between his understanding of mercy and ours. He called us to *change* the way we view and live out mercy.

- He made time for the beggar, outcast, and sick.
- He went out of his way for the woman at the well.
- He gave attention to the man at the Sheep Gate pool.
- He offered grace to the woman caught in adultery.

All of these perspectives required a shift in traditional thinking about the person Jesus gave his attention to—he didn't see them as pests, outcasts, or as less valuable to society. He viewed them as children of God, worthy of his attention, and he treated them as his friends.

When we begin to see need as an opportunity to live out the Gospel, we begin to see people differently. We'll put names with faces. And we'll hear stories we can relate with.

The heart of mercy changes things:

- True mercy changes judgment to humility.
- True mercy changes sympathy to action.
- True mercy changes our kingdom to God's Kingdom.
- True mercy changes selfishness to selflessness.
- True mercy changes doubt to faith.

*"I used to see the homeless community as a bunch of lazy people who probably got what they deserved. Then I began to hear their stories. I learned their names. And I realized that they weren't really all that different than me. For many, the only difference was that I had family to fall back on when times got tough. It took serving them for me to realize how much I had dehumanized them in my own mind. And it's exposed how big of a pattern that truly is in my life."* - John, a volunteer

## 3.3 NOTES

⊙ How do you think the way you view the "outcast, marginalized, or oppressed" differs from how God may view them?

⊙ Take a moment to think about the difference between sympathy and compassion as it relates to feeling and action. Write some of your thoughts below.

◯ Have you ever labeled a group of people unfairly? Where do you think that way of thinking comes from?

◯ What is the greatest shift you need to make in your thinking in order to grow a merciful heart toward the "least of these?" Hint: It starts in the heart.

## 3.4

## Do something intentional

When we first began to think about what it might mean to serve the least, we had no real idea what it might look like. But in order to cultivate a greater heart of mercy, we knew we had to do *something*.

So as a part of trying to gain a new understanding of Jesus' call for us to serve the least, we simply committed to do whatever popped up throughout the day. And we also purposefully considered the long-term impact of this shift of thinking.

If we take seriously the task of engaging need, it often starts with one thing and leads to another. *A heart of mercy* leads to *a concern for justice. The effort of learning* leads to *living it out. Being a blessing* leads to *the work of restoration*. Last week you made a commitment to being available to do whatever you accidentally happened upon. Today we want you to think about something you can *go out of your way to do*.

Here are some ideas to give you a head start: Call a local school and ask if there are any supplies they need, go buy them, and drop them off. Or search the "wanted" section on Craigslist for needs you can meet (often single moms and elderly people list needs there.)

Take a moment to brainstorm and come up with a brief list of five (reasonable) things you could do today if you decided to. Note them below to help you remember.

Now pick one and go do it! Simple or complex, just do something intentional that requires a heart of mercy and offers relief to a need with no guarantee of long-term impact.

### Brainstorm notes

# 3.5

**Plan for your community time** to be a little longer this week. There's lots to do! But first, enjoy a meal together. If there are kids, we've included a way for them to get involved too.

**Group Project:** Form an assembly line and complete your homeless packets first. This should be a meeting priority. For those of you choosing an alternative project that better suits your context, be sure to use the front end of your meeting to to do so and use whatever time is left for group discussion.

**Optional Kid Project**: In addition to the designated supplies from Community day 2.5, it might be a good idea to have someone bring supplies for kids to make cards for each of the homeless packets. These are a good idea if you're making these around a holiday and can be theme-oriented. But it's also a great way to involve the kids. (Note: Be sure to have someone guide them in what NOT to write. Keep it positive.)

- *Option #1:* Make the cards with your kids. Then complete the packets through an assembly line.
- *Option #2:* If you're short on time, have the kids make the cards in another room while you go through the discussion questions on the next page from this week's reading. Consider paying for child care to help with the kids so your whole group can be a part of the discussion.

MERCY_community

**Suggested questions for group discussion:**
On the first day (3.1), we talked a little about how a biblical view of mercy is more about an attitude of the heart. Share with the group what you wrote to the question, "What does a lack of love of mercy show us about our understanding of God's mercy?"

On day two (3.2), we see Jesus and the Old Testament prophet Hosea saying the same thing: "For I desire mercy, not sacrifice." In what ways should this apply to how we do church today?

On day four (3.4), we were challenged to make a list of things we could do if we put the effort forward. Share with the group what you did. If you didn't, share with the group your struggle.

**Follow through:** Divide up the homeless packets for group members to keep in their cars. As you see someone in need during the week, offer them a packet. If you have the kids in the car, have them roll down the window and do it from the back seat. Ask their names. Pray for them by name that evening with your kids. Take note of your kids' reactions.*

*For those of you choosing an alternative project for this week, be sure to delegate and designate responsibilities for following through. Don't forget to include the kids.

**Critical step for next week:** Go back to the list of non-profit organizations from Community day 2.5. Designate people to contact each one and find out how your group might serve what the organization is doing (specifically find out if there is a project or time your group could serve on week six). Be prepared to bring this back for discussion next week. This sometimes takes a little persistence. It might help to assign someone the job of checking in with everyone to make sure the contacts happen.

**3.6**

# Be good news to someone in need.

# Understanding mercy

One of the greatest tensions we will experience in serving others is navigating the distance between meeting temporary needs and having long-term impact. That's an honest concern that many share.

Not long ago I was having a conversation with a friend about some of our "relief" ministries related to serving the homeless. His response:

*"Feeding the homeless is just not for me. I'd prefer to create a sustainable ministry to help get them off the streets. Maybe develop a way to offer skills training. Something that's going to solve the problem not just offer a temporary solution."*

Great idea. In fact, I'd prefer that too. But here's a question: How's that going for you? Seriously. He had plenty of ideas, but he had literally no action. Many of us can relate. But what are we actually doing with our vision for this sustainable ministry?

For those out there creating long term programs...KUDOS! Great job. We need to work harder to support you and get involved. But the reality is, most of us know what needs to be done, yet do absolutely nothing.

We need to be ready for any opportunity and practice cultivating a heart of mercy. We're not going to solve hunger on the streets of our city through handing out a cheeseburger. We're not going to eradicate poverty by inviting a single mom to Thanksgiving dinner. But something will begin to change—I assure you this—and it will be us.

*"We need to stop clinging to the idea of being transformed and honestly, mournfully, and humbly ask him to break our hearts for the things that break his."* [from *Barefoot Church*]

When our heart changes and motivation comes from an understanding of mercy, our actions will come from the right place. Next week we'll get into the idea of having a longer-term impact. This week, just relax and think about what God might be doing through and in you as you just focus on being good news to someone in need of good news.

## 3.6 NOTES

◯ Have you ever served in a way where you felt what you were doing was temporary and possibly wasting your time? How could you view that service differently? How does God view his mercy shown to us in light of this?

◯ In what ways do you feel God cultivating a heart of mercy in you?

⬢ Do you feel like you are being transformed? Why or why not? What experiences would you say inform your answer the most?

⬢ Serving often takes one of two forms: Offering immediate relief or long-term relief. Which one appeals to you the most? In what ways do you believe one affects the other?

# 3.7

Therefore, I urge you, brothers, in view of God's mercy, to offer your bodies as living sacrifices, holy and pleasing to God—this is your spiritual act of worship. Do not conform any longer to the pattern of this world, but be transformed by the renewing of your mind. Then you will be able to test and approve what God's will is—his good, pleasing and perfect will. [Romans 12:1-2]

We are not trying to commend ourselves to you again, but are giving you an opportunity to take pride in us, so that you can answer those who take pride in what is seen rather than in what is in the heart. If we are "out of our mind," as some say, it is for God; if we are in our right mind, it is for you. ■ For Christ's love compels us, because we are convinced that one died for all, and therefore all died. And he died for all, that those who live should no longer live for themselves but for him who died for them and was raised again. ■ So from now on we regard no one from a worldly point of view. Though we once regarded Christ in this way, we do so no longer. Therefore, if anyone is in Christ, the new creation has come: The old has gone, the new is here!

[2 Corinthians 5:12-17]

MERCY_reCreate

**Consider this:** What if the evidence of a new heart is an ever increasing love of mercy? As we hold this question up to our life's motives and interactions, how do we stack up? Most of us have never prayed for a heart of mercy. If it's Christ's love that compels us, maybe now is a good time to start.

As you make room for rest, family and friends today, ask God to show you how he has demonstrated his mercy toward you through each person you come into contact with.

**WEEK 4**

# Justice

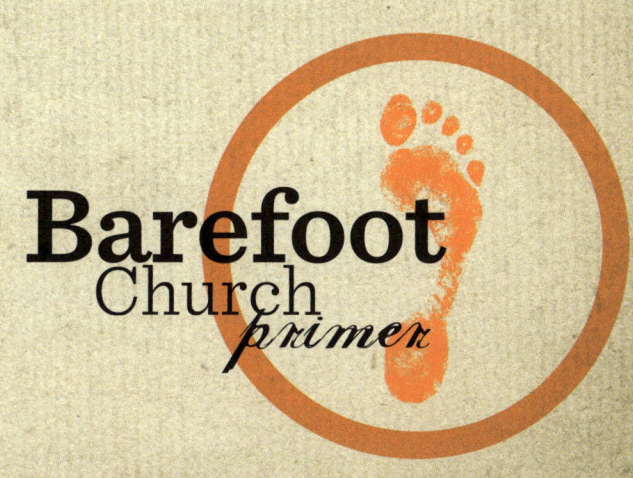

**4.1**

Simply put, mercy offers immediate and compassionate treatment of those in distress, and justice is the principle or ideal of just dealing or right action. Scripture clearly calls us to act justly and love mercy. Hopefully we can quickly move beyond the questions of "who and why" and on to the realities of "what, when, and how."   - from *Barefoot Church*

JUSTICE_exploration

## Seek justice

Last week, we discussed the heart of mercy as a motivator for compassionate action. Mercy moves us to respond with kindness to the needs that we see. It causes us to reach out to bring relief to places that are broken. But when we begin to act, mercy also begins to change us.

In the Hebrew language of the Bible, the definition for the word *justice* is: "To be made right, restored." Interestingly, the Hebrew word *tsedeq*, meaning "righteousness," is the same word used for *justice*. [Psalms 89:14; 23:3]

So justice is really about *righteous restoration*.

What's your definition of justice? Payback, retribution, punishment, getting even? Often we speak of "getting justice", the Bible speaks of "doing justice."

When we do justice, our hearts are aligned with the truth of the Gospel—which is that Christ died to make things right, to make them as they should be. Restored. When we act, participating in God's restorational justice, we begin to realize that this Gospel is bigger than any weekend service project. We intuitively begin to move from a ministry of relief to a ministry of restoration, from a "service project" to a new way of living, from the heart of mercy to the desire for true justice.

Engaging justice includes increased awareness, followed by an intentional and sustained effort to confront need as it appears in global forms such as the orphan crisis, human trafficking, or the need for clean water.

Mercy and justice together encompass the full Biblical concept of serving the least. An expression of mercy quickly becomes an act of justice when a need is engaged with the hope of a long-term solution. Mercy offers compassion and relief. Justice offers an advocate and action.

## 4.1 NOTES

◉ How does our initial discussion of justice match or contrast with the traditional perspective on justice? How is it shifting? Or is it?

◉ What are some ways that you feel an act of mercy differs from an act of justice? List them below.

◉ As you look at your life, God has filled it with many acts of mercy. (Remember, because of our sin we ultimately deserve death, so every good thing we have in our life is a display of God's mercy and grace toward us.) In what specific ways has his mercy begun to produce a heart of mercy in you, leading you to desire to do justice in your neighborhood or city?

# 4.2

## Think about it...

God is just. But his *justice* is expressed through his *mercy*. We see in the gift of Jesus the most perfect illustration of mercy translated into just action. God didn't have to send his son, but he did because of his love and mercy. ■ Our natural response to this is often that of a debtor, as if we could repay God. But that's not what he asks of us. He doesn't desire sacrifice—He's after something much deeper and more challenging than that. He wants our hearts.

With what shall I come before the LORD and bow down before the exalted God? Shall I come before him with burnt offerings, with calves a year old? ■ Will the LORD be pleased with thousands of rams, with ten thousand rivers of olive oil? Shall I offer my firstborn for my transgression, the fruit of my body for the sin of my soul? ■ He has shown you, O mortal, what is good. And what does the LORD require of you? To act justly and to love mercy and to walk humbly with your God. [Micah 6:6-8]

**Let's take a moment to revisit** the first chapter of Isaiah. God is literally calling his people a "rebellious nation" and that they don't even know it.

■ *I reared children and brought them up, but they have rebelled against me. The ox knows its master, the donkey its owner's manger, but Israel does not know, my people do not understand* [Isaiah 1:2-3].

■ The prophet goes on to express that their guilt is great. ■ *Woe to the sinful nation, a people whose guilt is great, a brood of evildoers, children given to corruption! They have forsaken the LORD; they have spurned the Holy One of Israel and turned their backs on him* (vs. 4). ■ Something had gone terribly wrong and it was impacting even the validity of their worship. It had driven a wedge between their efforts to please God and God's desire to be with them. ■ *Your offerings are meaningless. Your incense is detestable to me. I cannot bear your worthless assemblies. Your feasts and festivals I hate with all my being. When you pray, I hide my eyes from you* (vs. 13-15). ■ Then, in verse 17, he gives us the solution. ■ *Learn to do right; seek justice. Defend the oppressed. Take up the cause of the fatherless; plead the case of the widow.*

## 4.2 NOTES

◉ How does Micah's description of what God "requires" of us differ or fall in line with what you've always believed or been taught? How well would you say you've lived it?

◉ How has your response to "seeking justice" impacted your relationship with God? Why is that?

◐ How do you think the way the church today typically views mercy and justice affects how God views the church?




◐ How do you think the way the church today acts on issues of mercy and justice impacts how skeptics and the unbelieving view the church? How should this change?

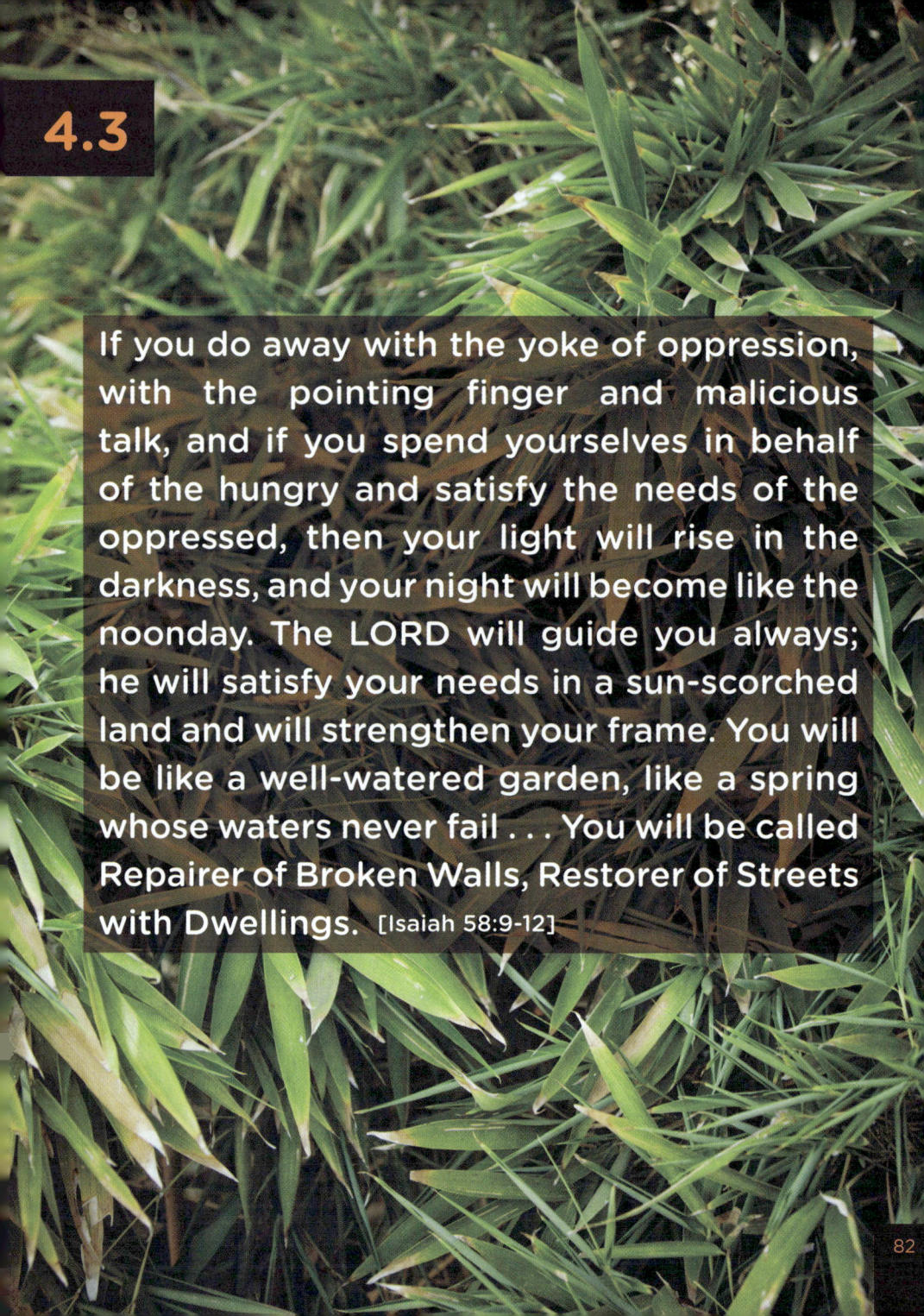

## 4.3

If you do away with the yoke of oppression, with the pointing finger and malicious talk, and if you spend yourselves in behalf of the hungry and satisfy the needs of the oppressed, then your light will rise in the darkness, and your night will become like the noonday. The LORD will guide you always; he will satisfy your needs in a sun-scorched land and will strengthen your frame. You will be like a well-watered garden, like a spring whose waters never fail . . . You will be called Repairer of Broken Walls, Restorer of Streets with Dwellings. [Isaiah 58:9-12]

## Cause and effect

We probably all struggle in varying degrees with *individualism, consumerism,* and *materialism.* All are barriers to the Kingdom. Thus, all are barriers to *justice.* We naturally prioritize our agendas by things that benefit us. Too often we live our lives on the brink and with nothing to spare that can be shared with others.

Even when we overcome those issues, we're often paralyzed by the worry that our efforts will fall short. We're concerned that the cost will be too great. We're not convinced that it's worth the work or that God really cares if we do.

But when we begin to understand that God values our heart and effort more than our success, how we view ourselves and our role in seeking justice will change dramatically. When that shift happens and we learn to value action for the right reason, just as we read in Isaiah 58, something amazing begins to take place.

## 4.3 NOTES

◆ Have you ever thought that individualism, consumerism, or materialism are all barriers to justice? Which do you struggle with the most? How so?

◆ Throughout scripture we're reminded that it's the heart God sees more than the success of our efforts. Why do you think this is an important thing to remember when we serve the least?

◯ Why do you think Isaiah reminds us that we will be called Restorers and Repairers when we serve the Least? What importance does that hold for the Kingdom?

◯ Do you think the church has the reputation of being an agent of restoration and repair? Why or why not? How can that begin to change?

## 4.4

## Close to home

As we gain a greater understanding of justice, we'll benefit most from simply taking action to serve others. In doing so, our eyes will begin to see things differently. We'll begin to see difficulties in serving, we'll begin to wrestle with different kinds of emotions that surface, and we'll begin to gain a better idea of how we naturally respond to it all, whether good or bad. All are necessary in ultimately finding a service "rhythm." None of that will happen without some intentional first steps.

Today we want you to turn back to Action day 2.4. where you were tasked to make a list of people in your community or neighborhood that have a need that you are aware of. Today, it's time to take action.

Choose one of the needs on the list that you can help with, be an encouragement about, or solve for them and do it.

This may not put you in a place where you are meeting a physical need, but it's still good practice and a helpful step in learning what it means to be good news. Plus, we'll gain the opportunity to learn from each other when we discuss for our day of community tomorrow.

JUSTICE_action

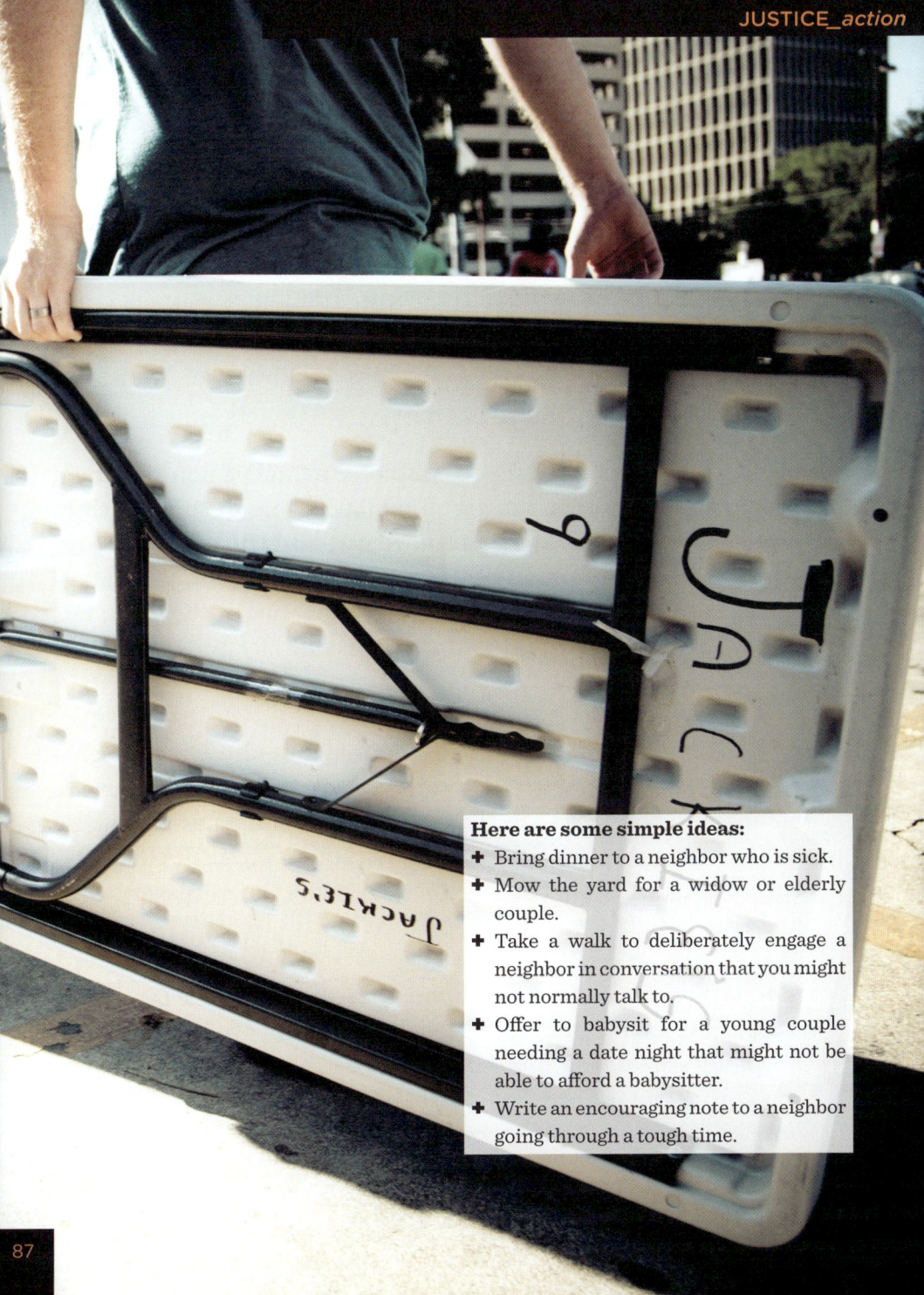

**Here are some simple ideas:**
+ Bring dinner to a neighbor who is sick.
+ Mow the yard for a widow or elderly couple.
+ Take a walk to deliberately engage a neighbor in conversation that you might not normally talk to.
+ Offer to babysit for a young couple needing a date night that might not be able to afford a babysitter.
+ Write an encouraging note to a neighbor going through a tough time.

## 4.5

- **Take a moment to go around the room and share stories from this week's day of Action.** Don't spend too much time on this, but make sure everyone gets a chance to share the "what, why, and how" of what they did.

- Last week you assigned people to contact the top five non-profits in your community that the group might be able to serve with in week six. **Discuss what you found out and the available options. Pick the one you feel is best for your group.** Remember that you can do this project any day between the week five and week seven community days. That literally gives you a two week window.

- **Talk about what you'll need to accomplish the task.** Decide who will do what. Write down follow up questions and assign a liaison to connect with the organization you'll be serving. Be willing to do whatever homework is required to make the project a reality. Make a commitment to make the necessary calls and emails right away (this is critical!)

    *Note:* Working with non-profits often requires flexibility. It's okay if the opportunity that you choose doesn't happen on your normally scheduled Community day. It's more important to pick something that the group might enjoy doing together and that can happen sometime during week six.

JUSTICE_*community*

**Suggested questions for group discussion:**
On the first day (4.1), we not only introduced the idea of justice from God's perspective, but we also exposed the idea that every good thing we have in our life is a display of God's mercy shown to us. Share with the group your answers to the question, "In what specific ways has his mercy begun to produce a heart of mercy in you, leading you to desire to do justice in your neighborhood or city?

How does Micah's description of what God "requires" of us differ or fall in line with what you've always believed or been taught? How well would you say you've lived it? (4.2)

Throughout scripture we're reminded that God is interested in our hearts more than the "success" of our efforts. Why do you think this is an important thing to remember when we serve the least? (4.3)

## 4.6

*Do not merely listen to the word, and so deceive yourselves. Do what it says.* ■ *Anyone who listens to the word but does not do what it says is like someone who looks at his face in a mirror* ■ *and, after looking at himself, goes away and immediately forgets what he looks like.* ■ *But whoever looks intently into the perfect law that gives freedom, and continues in it—not forgetting what they have heard, but doing it—they will be blessed in what they do.* ■ *Those who consider themselves religious and yet do not keep a tight rein on their tongues deceive themselves, and their religion is worthless.* ■ *Religion that God our Father accepts as pure and faultless is this: to look after orphans and widows in their distress and to keep oneself from being polluted by the world.* [James 1:22-27]

**By now you're probably** either experiencing a little excitement or even a little frustration. Usually it's one of the two extremes. This is normal. While most of us are wading in uncharted waters, we'd like to offer that the tension is worth wrestling with. In doing so, it's best for us to press deeper into why we're doing what we're doing.

Issues of justice are so big that it's easy to move from ignorance to paralysis. This adds to the tension because we can feel a bit helpless and even overwhelmed. Don't forget that God is just as interested in our obedience as the outcome. The future is in his hands, but what we do today is in ours.

JUSTICE_*calibration*

**"Charity is no substitute for justice withheld."** - Saint Augustine

**"At his best, man is the noblest of all animals; separated from law and justice he is the worst."** - Aristotle

## What if...

What if James *really meant* that the only religion that is acceptable to God is one that serves the orphan and widow? How does that change what we know about religion?

What if we took a serious look at what the Word says and hold it up to our lives to see what we're missing? How does that change the way we view ourselves?

What if we were to begin to fight injustice in the world? How would that change us?

What if it's true that Jesus came to preach the Gospel to the poor because they were the ones who would welcome and receive it? How would serving the least change the way the skeptical world viewed the church?

## 4.6 NOTES

◉ Have you ever felt paralyzed by the magnitude of need in the world? Describe how and why.

◉ Justice withheld is a new concept to many of us. Scripture claims that through our neglect, we become the oppressors. How does that make you feel? Why? What should you do about it?

⦿ Which of the "What If" questions do you resonate most with? Why?

⦿ Aristotle wrote: "At his best, man is the noblest of all animals; separated from law and justice he is the worst." What truths do you think motivated or inspired him to write this?

# 4.7

*We don't evaluate people by what they have or how they look. We looked at the Messiah that way once and got it all wrong, as you know.* ■ *We certainly don't look at him that way anymore. Now we look inside, and what we see is that anyone united with the Messiah gets a fresh start, is created new. The old life is gone; a new life burgeons! Look at it!* ■ *All this comes from the God who settled the relationship between us and him, and then called us to settle our relationships with each other. God put the world square with himself through the Messiah, giving the world a fresh start by offering forgiveness of sins.* ■ *God has given us the task of telling everyone what he is doing. We're Christ's representatives. God uses us to persuade men and women to drop their differences and enter into God's work of making things right.* [2 Corinthians 16-20, *The Message*]

# JUSTICE_reCreate

**Consider this:** Because of Christ's love for us, we will *not* receive what we deserve as a penalty for our sins (that's mercy), and we *have already* received forgiveness, eternal life, an indwelling Holy Spirit, and restored relationships with God and others (that's justice). Jesus did this. It is his work of mercy and justice expressed to us. We can rest in the knowledge that it will continue to be God's work and power that accomplishes justice in and through us to a world in need of restoration.

Spend some time in prayer today asking God to show you what false beliefs, fears, personal idols or selfish priorities you need to release.

# WEEK 5
# Expose

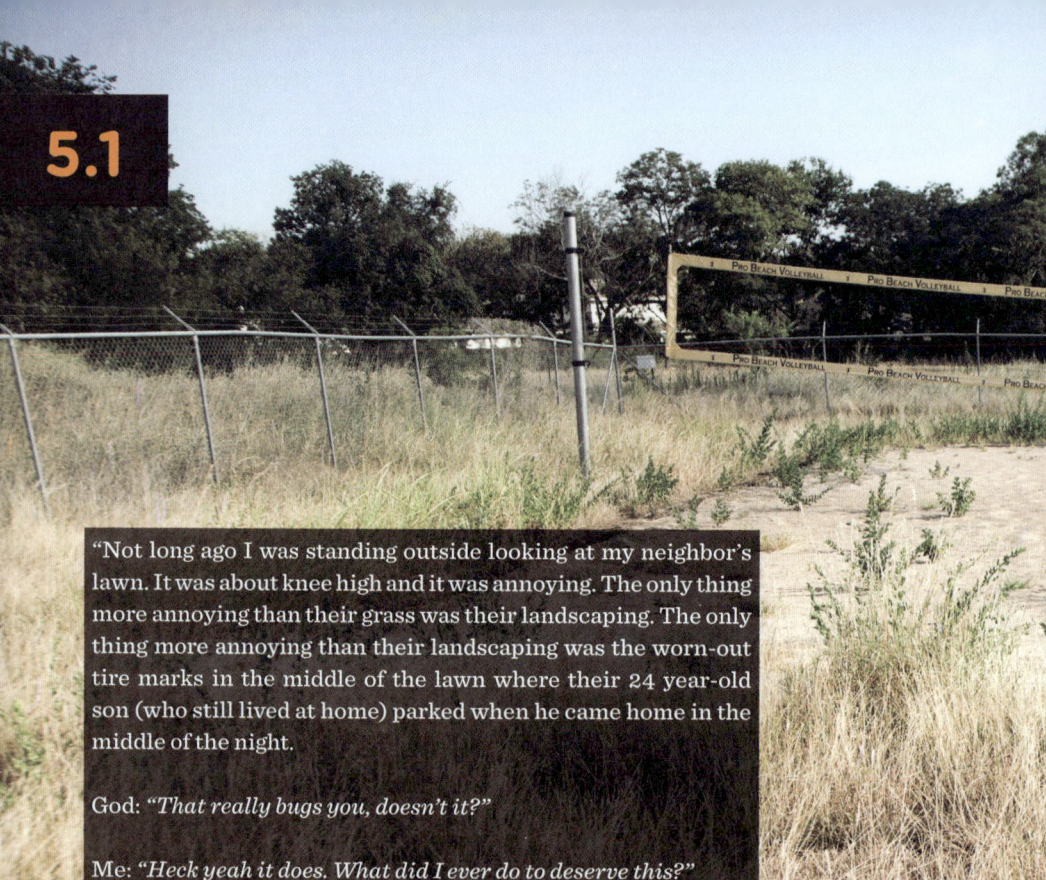

# 5.1

"Not long ago I was standing outside looking at my neighbor's lawn. It was about knee high and it was annoying. The only thing more annoying than their grass was their landscaping. The only thing more annoying than their landscaping was the worn-out tire marks in the middle of the lawn where their 24 year-old son (who still lived at home) parked when he came home in the middle of the night.

God: *"That really bugs you, doesn't it?"*

Me: *"Heck yeah it does. What did I ever do to deserve this?"*

God: *"Why don't you do something about it?"*

Me: *"Why would I? It's not my lawn."*

God: *"Because she's a widow who lost her husband five years ago to cancer and she doesn't know how to start a lawn mower. Because she's got a loser son who takes advantage of her day after day. Because you call yourself a Christ follower. Because you're so self-consumed that you didn't even see her need, and this is exactly what you need to do to change your heart."*

So I got out my lawnmower and started cutting. And I wept. And I did it every week. Both cut her lawn and cried. It took a whole five minutes. Quite the sacrifice. God made his point.

EXPOSE_*exploration*

## Three kinds of need

Mother Teresa taught that there are three kinds of needs in every community: *spiritual, physical* and *emotional*. ■ The deeper we look, the more need we'll see. We see physical poverty in our own cities and around the world, spiritual poverty among the religious as well as those who are not, emotional and relational poverty among the rich and poor alike. Whether it is across the ocean or across the street, need is everywhere. ■ The next three weeks we'll be committing our time to "exposing," "experiencing," and "engaging" need as an intentional process. This week we're learning to "expose" need through focusing on creating margin, practicing presence, and adjusting our priorities. Buckle up.

## 5.1 NOTES

◯ What would shift in your heart if you began to see every elderly woman as a mother—like your mother—and every single mom as your sister, and all children in need like they were your children? How would your priorities and motivation to serve them change?

◯ Consider Mother Teresa's thought about the three kinds of need in every community. Why is this a helpful starting point for us to serve?

◯ Why is it easier to see some types of need?

◯ What role do you think "looking for need" first could play in all of us beginning to "learn to do right"? What are the dangers of not looking before we jump?

## 5.2

## Blinded

Similar to yesterday's "lawn mowing" story, God's accusation against Israel was not just that they didn't "do justice," but that it *never even crossed their minds*. They didn't see the need of the widow who lived next door. And by their neglect, in the eyes of God, they became the oppressors. ■ *They do not defend the cause of the fatherless; the widow's case does not come before them.* [Isaiah 1:23] ■ Jesus spoke boldly about this problem. ■ *Woe to you, teachers of the law and Pharisees, you hypocrites! You give a tenth of your spices—mint, dill and cumin. But you have neglected the more important matters of the law—justice, mercy and faithfulness. You should have practiced the latter, without neglecting the former. You blind guides! You strain out a gnat but swallow a camel.* [Matthew 23:23-24] ■ Jesus reminds us that, in our religious pursuits, we can easily seek the wrong things. And become blind to the right things. But he also reminds us that when we seek the right things, we will find all that we're looking for (and then some). ■ *So I say to you: Ask and it will be given to you; seek and you will find; knock and the door will be opened to you. For everyone who asks receives; the one who seeks finds; and to the one who knocks, the door will be opened.* [Luke 11:9-10]

EXPOSE_*meditation*

"But seek first his kingdom and his righteousness, and all these things will be given to you as well." - Jesus

## 5.2 NOTES

◉ Have you ever missed seeing a need that was right under your nose? Why did you miss it?

◉ What did Jesus mean by accusing the religious of being "blind guides" and that they "strain out a gnat but swallow a camel?" What ways does this describe you?

◉ What has historically been your greatest hindrance to "seeking" what is right?

◉ Write a prayer of confession, asking God to reveal where you have allowed yourself to knowingly "be blind" to needs around you. Then ask him to show you what repentance in these areas looks like.

## 5.3

**Change always starts with a decision** which leads to action. If we are going to learn to express God's mercy and justice in our daily lives, we have to be willing to make the personal decisions which lead to change. One way to start is to identify the *distractions* present in our lives.

EXPOSE_change

# Making the right changes

### Margin
*Margin* is that space in your life in between "all the time in the world" and "the stuff I have to do." Many of us fill our days so full that we have very little margin, which means we rarely have time to talk to our neighbors, to engage the needs in our community, or to spend a few hours of "wasted time" with someone who is having a rough day. The lack of margin in our lives is one of the greatest enemies to mission. *Are there distractions in your daily life that eat up your margin and keep you from noticing the needs around you?*

### Presence
In an era of email, voicemail, Facebook, and text messaging, we sometimes forget the power of being physically present in people's lives. This absence is often the result of a lack of margin. It takes commitment and time to "be there," but it is a powerful way to communicate God's love. *What areas in your life are most impacted by the lack of your physical presence? Your family? Your work? Living on mission?*

### Priority
We set priorities and make decisions based on them every day. Unless being Good News becomes a true priority in our lives, we won't make the decisions necessary to create margin or commit to presence. *Now that we're in week five, it's a good time for a gut-check: Are you serious about this? Are you willing to move engaging need into the "stuff I have to do" category? Why or why not? What are you struggling with? Spend some time today talking to God about it.*

## 5.3 NOTES

◆ Write down the distractions that came to mind as you read the previous page. Which ones present the biggest challenge for you? Ask the Spirit to guide you in all of this.

◆ Which ones are the "easy ones?" Are there a few simple things that you could cut out of your life that would free up an hour here and there in your schedule? List them below.

◯ Are there relationships in your life that could benefit from you "being present?" Look for people who could especially use tangible Good News. What could you do to make time to be present with them?

◯ Let's take a timeout. Be honest with yourself and with God: How is this journey making you feel? What are you learning? How are you being stretched? Take some notes on where you're at (you might need an extra sheet of paper!)

## 5.4

Some statistics:

** 1 in 4 children go to bed hungry every night in central Texas.

** There are less than 300 adoptable kids in the foster system in the Austin area.

** There are more than 6000 homeless people in the Austin area and less than 300 dedicated shelter beds.

** Due to gentrification, the suburban poor in Austin now outnumber the urban poor.

** More than 50% of those under the poverty level in Austin are females with no husband present, 40% are married, and less than 10% are men.

** There are 1500 children in the Austin Independent School District who're listed as homeless.

** While Austin is constantly in the top five for number of non-profits in the US, we're not even in the top 30 for non-profit efficiency.

EXPOSE_*action*

# Be a student of your city

It took less than ten minutes online to find out the local stats listed on the previous page and about the same amount of time to find non-profits, cause groups, or benefit organizations working hard to address each need.

Take some time today to research the topics on the list below in your own area. Write down one significant statistic for each. Start with Google. Try city and county websites if you're having trouble.

**Homelessness:**

**Hunger:**

**Poverty:**

**Orphans/Foster Care:**

**Education:**

**Single Parents:**

**Human Trafficking:**

**The Elderly:**

**Add your own:**

## 5.5

* Yesterday, we were assigned to do some online research on needs in the community. Take some time to discuss what you found.

* Last week your group decided on a service project for week six. Give updates on the project. Reassign responsibilities if necessary and finalize any plans for when, how, and where you are meeting next week.

* Be clear and concise. Consider every angle. If your "serve" day is not on your normal community day, then make sure to figure out how that impacts your group meeting.

* Ask the question: *What are we forgetting?*

EXPOSE_community

**Suggested questions for group discussion:**
On the first day (5.1), we discussed the three types of need in every community as described by Mother Teresa (spiritual, physical, emotional). Discuss with the group your thoughts on her claim. Why are these helpful to think about as a community on mission together?

Discuss with the group what you think Jesus meant by accusing the religious of being "blind guides" and that they "strain out a gnat but swallow a camel." In what ways does this describe you? (5.2)

Share with the group your list of distractions (5.3).

From your research (5.4), share with the group which of the statistics you found to be most surprising or significant and why? How might God be leading you to respond to this information?

## 5.6

**If we were to truly adopt a holistic view of the Gospel,** our reason for serving would change. Our service would not be about us, it really wouldn't be about our individual church or faith community either. It could only be about the Kingdom. ■ The Kingdom breaks through any time and any place. God's way rules over our way. The Kingdom is exposed when we choose the way of Jesus. The Kingdom happens when we drop our agenda and serve like Jesus—selflessly. ■ Kingdom opportunities can literally be right in front of us, yet we run the risk of missing them. In places and societies of plenty, need is often hard to recognize. There are few third-world shanty towns springing up in our neighborhoods, and yet the need is often just as desperate. Unless we are intentionally watching for it, we can easily miss it and go obliviously on our way, continuing to do our outwardly religious activities. Our problem is most exposed when we do not see the need.

## Seen and not seen

Jesus said that the Kingdom is like a secret that not everyone understands. Even those who spent every day close to Jesus continued to miss it and had to ask him to explain further:

*The secret of the kingdom of God has been given to you. But to those on the outside everything is said in parables so that, "they may be ever seeing but never perceiving, and ever hearing but never understanding."* [Mark 4:11-12a]

## 5.6 NOTES

◉ Why do you think God continues to require us to seek so much when he could supernaturally give us clarity in an instant?

◉ How do you think serving the least opens our eyes to the Kingdom?

⊙ Why do you think we prefer to do outward acts of religion over the inward seeking of faith?

⊙ Some need we don't see because we're not looking. Some need we don't see because we are ignoring it. What percentage do you think we do of each? What does this tell us about ourselves?

## 5.7

## "They all ate and were satisfied."

Today we want to re-orient our hearts to help make sure our desires do not keep us from knowing the heart of God.

When Jesus heard what had happened, he withdrew by boat privately to a solitary place. Hearing of this, the crowds followed him on foot from the towns. ■ When Jesus landed and saw a large crowd, he had compassion on them and healed their sick. ■ As evening approached, the disciples came to him and said, "This is a remote place, and it's already getting late. Send the crowds away, so they can go to the villages and buy themselves some food." ■ Jesus replied, "They do not need to go away. You give them something to eat." ■ "We have here only five loaves of bread and two fish," they answered. ■ "Bring them here to me," he said. ■ And he directed the people to sit down on the grass. Taking the five loaves and the two fish and looking up to heaven, he gave thanks and broke the loaves. Then he gave them to the disciples, and the disciples gave them to the people. ■ They all ate and were satisfied, and the disciples picked up twelve basketfuls of broken pieces that were left over. ■ The number of those who ate was about five thousand men, besides women and children. [Matthew 14:13-21]

EXPOSE_reCreate

**Consider this:** God is still the One who shows us needs and is the ultimate provision for those needs.

Take some time today to thankfully reflect and rest in God's abundant provision in your life. It is out of the overflow of our gratefulness that we will find margin, become more intentionally present and begin to allow God to shift our priorities.

**WEEK 6**

# Experience

## 6.1

## Good intentions

*For the sinful nature desires what is contrary to the Spirit, and the Spirit what is contrary to the sinful nature. They are in conflict with each other, so that you do not do what you want.* [Galatians 5:17]

"You cannot think your way into a new kind of living. You have to live your way into a new kind of thinking." - Richard Rohr, author of *Simplicity*

**Even if we "expose" need** and we want to do something about it, there is still no guarantee we will take action and "experience" the need at any level. Good intentions can often remain just that. I'm sure you can relate. Deadlines are approaching, bills have to be paid, and school projects that require your help are waiting on the kitchen countertop.

We have some deeper issues, too. Beyond being unmotivated and unconvinced, the big issue is that our flesh literally opposes it. In other words, without a transformed heart, we simply don't want to serve. It's a difficult truth, but it's good to be honest with ourselves and know our starting point.

We feel sympathy for those in need. But it's the Holy Spirit within us that leads and enables us to act. We often can't change the way we feel. But we can take a step and trust that the Spirit will empower and transform us. And as we act, we move into a new place of experiencing the need around us in new ways.

## 6.1 NOTES

◉ What benefit is there to simply trying or "experiencing" something you might not normally experience? While it sounds a bit simple, what can we learn from this method of exploration?

◉ What are the things you've used as seemingly legitimate reasons to NOT do more good that were really excuses?

◆ What are the things you've used as seemingly legitimate reasons to NOT do more good that are truly legitimate reasons? What can you learn from those things?

◆ Why is it good to understand the battle between flesh and spirit? How should this change the way we engage the battle?

## 6.2

*Taste and see that the LORD is good; blessed is the one who takes refuge in him.* ■ *Fear the LORD, you his holy people, for those who fear him lack nothing.* ■ *The lions may grow weak and hungry, but those who seek the LORD lack no good thing.* ■ *Come, my children, listen to me; I will teach you the fear of the LORD.* ■ *Whoever of you loves life and desires to see many good days,* ■ *keep your tongue from evil and your lips from telling lies.* ■ *Turn from evil and do good; seek peace and pursue it.* ■ *The eyes of the LORD are on the righteous, and his ears are attentive to their cry;* ■ *but the face of the LORD is against those who do evil, to blot out their name from the earth.* ■ *The righteous cry out, and the LORD hears them; he delivers them from all their troubles.* ■ *The LORD is close to the brokenhearted and saves those who are crushed in spirit.* [Psalm 34:8-18]

EXPERIENCE_*meditation*

## Experience needed

For some of us, God's call in Psalm 34 is a surprising one and uniquely compassionate. "Taste and see," he says, inviting us to experience even before we are convinced that's what we should be doing. As our creator, he knows us and understands the power of direct experience. And if we respond, what we end up experiencing is more than we could have ever imagined.

In the same way, he calls us to experience the need around us through seeking to meet that need. We may see it and even have a desire to take action. But it's often not until we experience it personally that we really start to "get it."

## 6.2 NOTES

⊙ What does God's invitation for us to "taste and see" tell you about him?

⊙ Psalm 34 says that the Lord is close to the brokenhearted. What does that teach you about proximity and need?

◯ Take a moment to consider God as creator: He knows even more than we do what we need to experience. How does that impact or change how you might approach learning to serve?

◯ Have you ever tried something for the first time that you never imagined you would like, but you did? What did you learn from that experience? Why do you think it's so easy to allow that line of thinking to remain as an isolated experience?

# 6.3

## Setting our priorities

**We need to dramatically shift our thinking** about what a service *event* accomplishes. We've pretty much conditioned ourselves to be able to consume anything—even a service event. Let's not throw out the baby with the bathwater, because there are some great uses for event-based service projects. But we have to keep a new perspective in mind as we do them.

### Old School
The event itself is the end goal of planning.

A one-time service event is all God requires.

We all go back to our normal lives when the event is done.

The event is something that stands alone as a part of doing church.

### New School
The event is the means for engaging need on a deeper level.

A one-time service event is something God uses to shape our hearts for more significant things.

We are all challenged to ponder what we're learning, how it should impact how we live, and what more we could do.

The event is an opportunity to reveal the service as a significant part of being the Church.

EXPERIENCE_*change*

*We tell our people to go. We tell them to be good news. And we assume they do. We assume they know how. While we've been charged as leaders to "equip the saints" for works of service, the brutal truth is that most of us have reduced our expectations of "serving" to a once-a-month tour of duty as an usher or greeter. We've settled for serving ourselves and serving as an event, rather than serving those in need and as a new way of life that Jesus called us to.*

[from *Barefoot Church*]

## 6.3 NOTES

◆ What ways do you think we can "consume" a service project or event? How do we move from consumers to contributors?

◆ How does thinking about a service event or project as a conduit for engaging more need change the way you might choose the project itself?

◆ Have you ever done a service project for completely selfish reasons? Thinking about that, how does it make you feel about future opportunities to serve?

◆ In what ways do you most need to change in the way you view a service event?

# 6.4

"Who is going to harm you if you are eager to do good? But even if you should suffer for what is right, you are blessed."

— Paul

EXPERIENCE_*action*

# Final preparation

Have your project leader send out a group email with an update on the project. Be sure to list all the responsibilities for the upcoming group project. This is a good day to "over-communicate."

Be sure to *Reply To All* with updates and changes.

Commit this day to accomplishing the tasks assigned to you.

Spend some time in prayer for the project:

+ That God would open your eyes to greater need.
+ That God would help you to connect the dots between serving the needy and developing community.
+ That God would eliminate any fears you have.
+ That God would expose any blind spots in your project.
+ That God would eliminate your expectations and enable you to serve completely without selfish motives.
+ That God would teach you in success.
+ That God would teach you in failure.
+ That God would be the only one who gains glory for this event.

Be encouraged and have fun. It might be a good idea to plan ahead to be flexible on this first event. Serving can be messy and rarely goes as planned. Don't expect it to go on without a hitch and don't forget that the effort in itself can be a huge win!

# 6.5

**This is the week** we take collective action. The plans of the last couple weeks should have prepared you for your first project together.

Be sure to plan on grabbing dinner together or plan something else to simply hang out after your project. Debrief. Spend some time discussing the project and anything that you learned in the process. List a few of them in the space provided.

Relax. Keep it simple. Enjoy one another's company. And be sure to celebrate something new!

EXPERIENCE_community

Notes

EXPERIENCE_calibration

# Connecting the dots

Serving those in need has a broader impact than you might think. Something happens when we are committed to doing what is right. Sometimes it even serves as the catalyst for connecting the dots on things we've been struggling with for years:

In September of 2008, Hurricane Ike hit the Texas coast and Austin quickly became the home to thousands of refugees in need. Within 24 hours of the hurricane hitting, our community was hosting 82 complete strangers in our various houses. It was the best thing that ever happened to our young church.

Not once did I feel personally put out. Not once that week did anyone complain about their plans being cancelled to serve those in need. No one worried about the children's ministry check-in process. No one complained that they had to give their time. They just gave. All they could. They gave without coercion or guilt.

The next Sunday's worship gathering was simply amazing. Everyone, literally everyone, who was a part of ANC was in attendance. The Spirit was thick. The worship was pure. The sharing was raw. Everyone was thankful for what they had and thankful to be able to give. Undoubtedly, it was the most intuitively worshipful gathering we had ever had.

In a world where we're constantly asking what went wrong, I couldn't help but ask: What went right?

What we found is that mission directly impacts the gathering. What we do on Monday through Saturday has everything to do with the spirit and heart of our Sundays.

## 6.6 NOTES

⊙ Why do you think worship was impacted so much by our week of crisis?

⊙ Have you ever had an experience that caused you to completely change the way you viewed something spiritually? What was it?

◗ Take a moment to consider the early church. What impact did their great need and persecution have on how they cared for one another? How do you think that impacted God's presence among them?

◗ What can we learn about the role of experiencing need as an agent for fostering community?

## 6.7

*Come, you who are blessed by my Father; take your inheritance, the kingdom prepared for you since the creation of the world.* ■ *For I was hungry and you gave me something to eat, I was thirsty and you gave me something to drink, I was a stranger and you invited me in, I needed clothes and you clothed me, I was sick and you looked after me, I was in prison and you came to visit me.* ■ *Then the righteous will answer him, "Lord, when did we see you hungry and feed you, or thirsty and give you something to drink? When did we see you a stranger and invite you in, or needing clothes and clothe you? When did we see you sick or in prison and go to visit you?"* ■ *The King will reply, "Truly I tell you, whatever you did for one of the least of these brothers and sisters of mine, you did for me."* [Matthew 25:34-40]

EXPERIENCE_reCreate

**Consider this:** Often when we serve others we don't necessarily feel like doing it, or we think that it was not that big of a deal. Sometimes we serve with great passion and the ones being served are not really that thankful.

Jesus reminds us that whatever and whenever we serve someone in great need, it is like we are serving him. Believing Jesus' teaching on this rewires our hearts to rest in the knowledge that Jesus is served and the Father is glorified every time we serve the least among us.

**WEEK 7**

*Engage*

## 7.1

### Asking the tough questions

After going through the exercise of *exposing* the need around us and allowing our hearts to *experience* it through the lens of community, we come to a challenging question: *What do we do next?*

That's exactly where we found ourselves as a community. The service events were great. But it was too easy to go back to our normal lives and remain unchanged. And while we were certainly *good news* to a bunch of people who needed good news, the long-term impact of what we were doing seemed very small. Was this really a full expression of God's justice? Would it bring true restoration in people's lives? Would anyone come to faith in Jesus because of our little projects?

ENGAGE_*exploration*

*During the first year of our community we would frequently load up the trailers for a grill-out downtown with the homeless community of Austin.* ■ *It was a fun event. We'd hand out more than 300 hot cheeseburgers, bags of chips, and bottles of water. The more we came, the more people we knew, and the easier the conversation was. Everyone was beginning to "feel" what we were searching for.* ■ *One weekend there was a new visitor to our grill-out. She was a homeless single mom, pushing a stroller, with a baby in it and a toddler hanging off the back. Behind her were two more children running along trying to keep up as she found her place in line.* ■ *Of all the people in line, it just seemed wrong that she was out there. It was over 100 degrees that day. And it was amazing to see our people step up.* ■ *That "event" became the conduit for engaging need on a different level. Over the next several months our people walked with her to get her off the streets and obtain the assistance she needed. I wish I could tell you it was easy. It wasn't. But what I can tell you is that everyone involved was radically changed.* ■ *Including the young mom. She was the first person ever baptized at our church.* [from *Barefoot Church*]

## 7.1 NOTES

◉ Take a moment to think about a service project you've done in the past. Were there opportunities to engage need on a deeper level that you missed? As you look back now, why did you miss them?

◉ Do you have a hard time trusting that service will lead to greater things? Why or why not?

◉ What does that say about what you believe the value of service really is? Is your belief more influenced by church culture, your personal history, or scripture? Explain.

◉ How much do you think engaging need is about the person being served and/or the person serving? Explain your answer.

◉ How is serving those in need a display of the Gospel?

## 7.2

# Learning to trust

To engage is to fully commit. It carries with it the expectation of focused effort and the idea that we're embarking on something that might require all we've got—spiritually, physically, and emotionally.

Seeking justice—moving beyond acts of simple mercy—requires that we engage at a much deeper and intentional level. This is often the point where we start to struggle. We do something good, but we fall short of the goal and the result is a season of doubt, confusion, or even frustration at ourselves and at the injustice God seems to tolerate.

This is the point where Jesus calls us to carefully consider the cost in our own lives, step forward in faith, and enter the life of a disciple, learning to trust in him. When we do this, we can be sure that God is with us and that God is working in us.

> "What, then, shall we say in response to these things? If God is for us, who can be against us?" [Romans 8:31]

ENGAGE_*meditation*

Surely God is good to Israel, to those who are pure in heart. ■ But as for me, my feet had almost slipped; I had nearly lost my foothold. ■ For I envied the arrogant when I saw the prosperity of the wicked. ■ From their callous hearts comes iniquity; their evil imaginations have no limits. ■ They scoff, and speak with malice; with arrogance they threaten oppression. ■ This is what the wicked are like—always free of care, they go on amassing wealth. ■ Surely you place them on slippery ground; you cast them down to ruin. ■ How suddenly are they destroyed, completely swept away by terrors! ■ They are like a dream when one awakes; when you arise, Lord, you will despise them as fantasies. ■ When my heart was grieved and my spirit embittered, ■ I was senseless and ignorant; I was a brute beast before you. ■ Yet I am always with you; you hold me by my right hand. ■ You guide me with your counsel, and afterward you will take me into glory. ■ Whom have I in heaven but you? ■ And earth has nothing I desire besides you. ■ My flesh and my heart may fail, but God is the strength of my heart and my portion forever. ■ Those who are far from you will perish; ■ you destroy all who are unfaithful to you. ■ But as for me, it is good to be near God. ■ I have made the Sovereign LORD my refuge; I will tell of all your deeds. [selections from Psalm 73]

## 7.2 NOTES

◉ How do you think a life truly committed to service would change you? What are your greatest struggles, fears or emotional inhibitors to serving? List them below.

◉ What would have to change in your life if it were to become radically reoriented around God's mission, service to others and making disciples? Think through the different areas of your life: time with family, friends, work, entertainment, resource allocation, etc.

◎ How does the good news of Jesus' life, death and resurrection on your behalf speak to any fears or barriers you may have?

◎ After reading Psalm 73, what is the thing about God that stands out most to you?

# 7.3

## Setting your priorities

As apprentices of Christ we need to take responsibility for engaging need on our own. It's unbiblical and ineffective for us to sit on the sidelines expecting others to plan service events for us. There's a huge difference between consuming and contributing. Until we shift our thinking and take initiative to engage need, we will always be consumers of the event. Worse still, we won't experience the maturity and unity that scripture promises will follow.

*"So Christ himself gave the apostles, the prophets, the evangelists, the pastors and teachers, to equip his people for works of service, so that the body of Christ may be built up until we all reach unity in the faith and in the knowledge of the Son of God and become mature, attaining to the whole measure of the fullness of Christ."* [Ephesians 4:11b-13]

Paul himself taught that we need a paradigm shift in our leadership and discipleship process. People seem to believe that the leadership gifts of the church are given so pastors can serve the believers. But Paul was clear to communicate the gifts were to be used to equip the believers to serve.

### Paradigm Shift

| | |
|---|---|
| Pastors serving the congregation | Pastors equipping the congregation to serve |
| People learning about Jesus | People learning to live on mission for Jesus |
| Pastors providing service programs and events | Pastors exposing need and people engaging need |
| Pastors trying to motivate people to grow spiritually | People taking initiative for their own personal growth |

## ENGAGE_change

## The benefits

"Then we will no longer be infants, tossed back and forth by the waves, and blown here and there by every wind of teaching and by the cunning and craftiness of people in their deceitful scheming. Instead, speaking the truth in love, we will grow to become in every respect the mature body of him who is the head, that is, Christ. From him the whole body, joined and held together by every supporting ligament, grows and builds itself up in love, as each part does its work." [Ephesians 4:14-16]

## 7.3 NOTES

◆ Have you ever held the mindset that it was the pastor's job to serve the church more than it was to equip the church? How has that impacted your faith experience?

◆ In what ways have you taken initiative for meeting needs you see in your community?

◆ In what ways have you taken initiative for your own spiritual growth?

◆ What does your answer to the last two questions tell you about how you've viewed your responsibility as a part of the church? Is that good or bad?

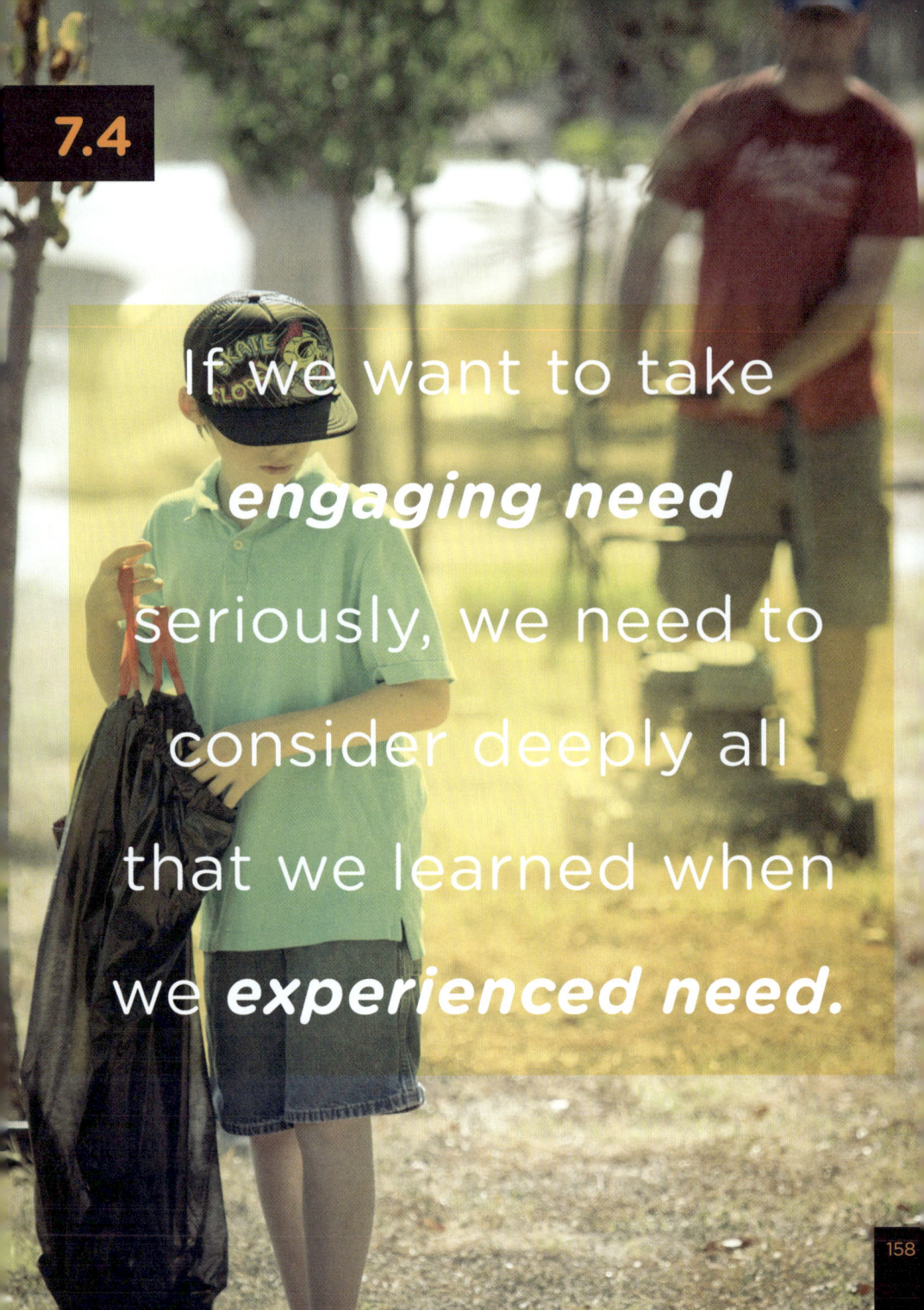

**7.4**

If we want to take *engaging need* seriously, we need to consider deeply all that we learned when we *experienced need.*

ENGAGE_*action*

Take a moment to consider additional needs that were exposed during last week's project that you, another individual, or your group might be able to engage. List them below.

On Community day in week four (day 4.5), you considered service projects with five different non-profit organizations. Consider the other projects you chose *not* to do. With the experience that you gained last week, take some notes on the needs you might expect to find in those other projects. Think about what it might look like to *engage* there.

**Project**                                          **Possible Needs**

*Scripture reminds us to "count the cost" of following Jesus. Take a moment now to go back over your list and rate their difficulty on a scale of 1-10 (10 being the most difficult).*

# 7.5

**Last week your group took part** in a service project and hopefully spent a little time debriefing. Now that you've had a few days to think about the project, take a moment as a group to evaluate it. Discuss the following questions:

* How effective was the project itself?
* Was it a good fit for the skills and interests of your group?
* Did it help to expose your group to greater need?
* How might serving build relationships that lead to making disciples?
* Did it provide opportunities to go deeper?
* Did it help you to grow or give you new insight?
* Was it a good opportunity to simply be "good news"?

Yesterday for our Action day (7.4), we were tasked with developing a list of opportunities to engage need at the next level. Discuss your list with the group and consider how you might best deal with each opportunity. Take notes below on next steps and assign tasks to individuals or teams for next week's day of Action (8.4). Be sure and choose the most "doable" actions. At this point in the journey, it's better to do something simple that you can actually accomplish.

| Assignment | Person responsible |
|---|---|
|   |   |

ENGAGE_community

**Suggested questions for group discussion:**
Do you have a hard time trusting that a service project will lead to greater things? Why or why not? (7.1)

On day two of this week (7.2), we were challenged to make a list of our greatest struggles or inhibitors to serving. Share with the group your greatest concern.

Share with the group your answer to the following question from day three of this week: Have you ever held the mindset that it was the pastor's job to serve the church more than it was to equip the church? How has that belief impacted your faith experience?

## 7.6

## Discipleship through serving

We typically think about the idea of serving as a *duty* of any Christ follower. But according to scripture, the heart of service is not just something we do, it is part of our new identity in Christ. It is part of who we are. Jesus said, *"I am among you as one who serves."* All those who follow Jesus are called to serve in the same humility. Jesus was a servant, and if we are his apprentices, then we are servants too. When we see serving "the least" as a basic element of our new identity, it can become one of the greatest catalysts for life change.

*That, however, is not the way of life you learned* ■ *when you heard about Christ and were taught in him in accordance with the truth that is in Jesus.* ■ *You were taught, with regard to your former way of life, to put off your old self, which is being corrupted by its deceitful desires;* ■ *to be made new in the attitude of your minds;* ■ *and to put on the new self, created to be like God in true righteousness and holiness."* [Ephesians 4:20-24]

**When Jesus told us** to go and make disciples, he was describing a new way of life. Yet most of us do not feel new. Many of us feel like we're on a hamster wheel when it comes to spiritual growth and nothing is changing. We're learning a lot, but we're not experiencing an equal amount of transformation.

Let's be honest for a moment. Knowing what we know about God, is there any reason to doubt that he wants us to serve the poor? Is there any chance our lack of doing so negatively impacts our spiritual development? Or that doing so would radically increase it?

Take a moment to consider these scriptures: does God desire that we be agents of peace [Matthew 5:9], ministers of reconciliation [2 Corinthians 5:18-19], and agents of renewal [Colossian 3:10]? Should we fight for the orphan [James 1:27] and plead the case of the widow [Isaiah 1:17]? Does he really want us to fight injustice [Isaiah 58:6]? Should we show mercy [Matthew 5:7]?

Considering these questions honestly, it becomes clear that if we are to be true disciples of Christ, our value of mission must increase.

## 7.6 NOTES

◉ Have you ever felt like you're not being "transformed," yet you're doing everything you're supposed to do and seemingly checking every spiritual box? What does that tell you about where you find your indentity?

◉ How does the idea of letting go of your agenda and taking on the identity (who you are known as) of a servant impact you?

◐ Have you ever considered that Jesus told us to serve the poor for more reasons than one? Why or why not? How have your views changed over the past several weeks?

◐ Does the amount of scripture that seems to enforce the idea of engaging need as a way of life surprise, affirm, confuse, or challenge you more? Which ones and why?

# 7.7

> In your relationships with one another, have the same mindset as Christ Jesus:
>
> Who, being in very nature God, did not consider equality with God something to be used to his own advantage; rather, he made himself nothing by taking the very nature of a servant, being made in human likeness.
>
> And being found in appearance as a man, he humbled himself by becoming obedient to death—even death on a cross!
>
> Therefore God exalted him to the highest place and gave him the name that is above every name, that at the name of Jesus every knee should bow, in heaven and on earth and under the earth, and every tongue acknowledge that Jesus Christ is Lord, to the glory of God the Father. [Philipians 2:5-11]

ENGAGE_reCreate

**Consider this:** Sometimes our acts of service, if we are honest, can be more about us *looking good* than about Jesus and his glory. That not only puts the focus completely in the wrong place but it also puts SO MUCH pressure on us to perform! What an endless treadmill our life will become if we do not learn to rest in the truth of our new identity as a servant, and live out of that knowledge and freedom.

Take a moment to prayerfully meditate on this reality. Confess where you might take credit. Pray for perspective. And thank God for his liberating truth.

**WEEK 8**

# The Intuitive Life

# 8.1

If you love me, keep my commands. And I will ask the Father, and he will give you another advocate to help you and be with you forever—the Spirit of truth. [John 15:15-17]

THE INTUITIVE LIFE_*exploration*

## Finding our rhythm

So here we are starting our last week together. By this point, you've probably begun to wrestle with the reality of the challenge, struggles, and sacrifice it takes to really live a consistent life of Gospel good news.

But you've probably also had moments, both personally and collectively, where things have started to make sense and where the Gospel in all its richness has pointed you in new directions.

We hope that if you remember anything from this study, it is that serving must become a part of our natural rhythms of life. This only happens when we train our hearts to listen to the Holy Spirit and create enough margin and time to be obedient to what we hear. This is what we mean by living the *intuitive life*.

Guided by the Spirit, our life and experience as part of a community will continue to grow and become more naturally attuned to this way of living. You will begin to see opportunity all around you and serve in the strength offered by God through his very own Spirit!

## 8.1 NOTES

◆ Does living life in a community on mission feel like a natural rhythm to you? Why or why not? What are you learning about yourself?

◆ What do you think is going on in your heart and life when you don't feel like serving or are not wanting to be a part of community?

◉ Where should the motivation and strength to continue come from? How does that make a difference?

◉ In what ways has serving together impacted your community group?

◉ Why do you think it takes intentional repetition for something to become more intuitive? What does that tell you about what you need to do in the coming weeks?

# 8.2

"Eventually, we've all got to deal with the reality of our biblical responsibility to serve those in need and it's essential impact on our faith journey. It changes the scorecard on how we should view faithfulness as a Christ follower."

**But the Bible is not calling us to just take our best guess** at what this life should look like and then work hard at it. Scripture shows us that Jesus' life, and the life of his followers, was completely guided by the indwelling Holy Spirit. We need to know how God wants us to live each day in the context he has placed us in.

*These are the things God has revealed to us by his Spirit. The Spirit searches all things, even the deep things of God. For who knows a person's thoughts except their own spirit within them? In the same way no one knows the thoughts of God except the Spirit of God. What we have received is not the spirit of the world, but the Spirit who is from God, so that we may understand what God has freely given us. This is what we speak, not in words taught us by human wisdom but in words taught by the Spirit, explaining spiritual realities with Spirit-taught words. The person without the Spirit does not accept the things that come from the Spirit of God but considers them foolishness, and cannot understand them because they are discerned only through the Spirit.* [1 Corinthians 2:10-14]

## 8.2 NOTES

◉ If we are a Christian, the Bible teaches we have the Holy Spirit dwelling within us. How should this affect our ability to live an intuitive life?

◉ In reality, God is always out on mission with you. How does that make you feel?

◉ In Romans 8 it says that the Holy Spirit was the power that raised Jesus from the dead. How does that level of "power" living inside of us speak to our fears or lack of strength?

◉ How does that level of power affect the connection between our faith and action?

# 8.3

## Created for good works

You may not realize this, because it seems like our journey together is just about done, but we are at a critical point in the process. This is where the rubber must meet the road. If all we do is a one-time service event, our efforts will continue to be about us.

Jesus said, "I am the way, and the truth and the life." He did not say, "I am the way and the truth and the EVENT."

**If we take time to listen to the Spirit,** we'll see needs all around us. We'll begin to learn how to actually live an intuitive life of a disciple who embodies the good news.

*But the Advocate, the Holy Spirit, whom the Father will send in my name, will teach you all things and will remind you of everything I have said to you.* [John 14:26]

This requires a huge shift in thinking for many of us. Instead of either neglecting the clear call to love mercy and do justice in the world, or trying to perform a long list of things in our own strength (often things God never asked us to do) we keep the motivation, plans, strength and outcomes of the mission ultimately as God's responsibility. We move beyond the thought that we are here to just "suffer and survive" this world, waiting for Jesus to come back and take us to Heaven. We respond obediently to the Word and Spirit as a way of life, right here and right now.

## 8.3 NOTES

⊙ Think back to our discussion on "learning to do right" (1.6) How does seeing the Holy Spirit as your indwelling teacher encourage you?

⊙ This thing is probably bigger than we know. How do you think serving the least can actually become a way to "preach the Gospel" that ultimately leads to people trusting in Jesus?

◗ What are some ways you've learned over the past several weeks to break out of the "serving as an event" mentality?

◗ As a believer, have you ever held the "suffer and survive this world" mentality? What gave you this mindset? What things other than serving would be impacted by a shift away from this way of thinking?

# 8.4

## Making good decisions

During our Community day (7.5) last week, we were assigned "next steps" to engage any needs that were exposed during our service experience. If you haven't already, take a moment today to follow up on your assignment. Whatever needs to be done, take a first step, asking the Spirit to guide you. Write down what you did.

During week 5 (day 5.3), we were challenged to create *margin* in our lives in order to clear away the things that might distract us from living out the Good News. We were challenged to make specific decisions that could lead to change.

Over the past few weeks, we've begun to experience the practical realities of caring for the needs that are revealed around us. It's a good time to re-examine the margin we have built into our lives.

Take some time today to consider the questions on the next page. Pray for the Spirit to guide your thoughts. Listen for his voice.

THE INTUITIVE LIFE_*action*

What must you say "NO" to in order to live a more Intuitive Life?

What must you say "YES" to in order to live a more Intuitive Life?

## 8.5

## Wrapping up & looking ahead

We hope that by now you've picked up some practical ideas for engaging need through incarnational community as well as gaining a deeper understanding of God's work of mercy and justice in the world. Additionally, you are hopefully learning to increasingly trust the Holy Spirit to guide and empower your efforts together.

While this is the last week of the study, it certainly doesn't need to be the last of your serving. While every group will look different, we think there are a handful of things you can do to make sure your community continues to have a focus and make an impact outside itself.

Together with your group, consider the suggestions we've listed on the facing page.

**Make a schedule for serving regularly together.**
Maybe it's just a once a month project that you all commit to. Or maybe it's an ongoing serving relationship with a local non-profit. The key is to make sure you create the organizational structure to ensure you do something. It might be a good idea to replace a regular community time with serving time. It might even keep things fresh. Be sure to grab dinner afterwards for a time to debrief. If your schedules are too tight even for that, we suggest you re-read the bit about *margin*.

**Appoint a service coordinator.**
Draw straws, elect, or beg for a volunteer from your group whose only job is to make sure you serve according to your plan (we recommend serving together at least once a month). Give this person a few minutes at the beginning of each community gathering to discuss some options and to plan effectively.

**Don't give up!**
Some of you may not have had a great service experience with your first project. That's pretty common. Remember, success isn't just having a great event, it's a Spirit-guided journey together into God's will. Choose one of the other non-profits you researched and try again! Keep doing this until you find one you can stick with or you see a more intuitive need you can engage more regularly (and remember the journey).

## 8.6

# Living in the tension

Let's talk about something that everyone feels but is rarely addressed in the world of serving the least: *tension*.

When we hold our lives up to an ideal, it causes tension. When we are confronted with cost of doing a good thing, it causes tension. Especially when we have to give up stuff we like for stuff that seems to just create more tension.

In moments like these, it's helpful to remember that this tension can have a good effect. Whether it serves to simply steady us or create a moment of self-examination in which we consider our position and check our motives, tension always comes with an opportunity for growth.

In fact, tension is often a sign that God is at work in our lives.

But be careful, when we focus only on eliminating tension, our focus turns inward and becomes selfish. We search for relief from the feelings rather than seeking growth and change.

Jesus said, "My yoke is easy and my burden is light." If the tension we feel becomes unbearable, or causes us to stress out, then there is a good chance that we are under a self-made yoke—not the yoke of Jesus.

THE INTUITIVE LIFE_*calibration*

*I'd like to take a more optimistic view . . . that the tension does not go away, we don't necessarily get over the hump, but the Spirit changes the way we view tension. We can take pleasure in tension when it comes from 'wanting to want to do something good.' [This is] one of the reasons we need to do it in community . . . we're in it together, we can remind each other what is right. We're there for each other in our moment of need, doubt, and struggle. And we find our joy in those relationships.*

- Jeff Vanderstelt

*There is a tendency in American Christianity to think we can choose a path without tension. Most of us would prefer to chart our journey that way. But God has called us to join his journey—one that is more amazing, wonderful, scary, awesome, engaging, dangerous, passionate, and rewarding than anything we could ever dream of.* - from *Barefoot Church*

## 8.6 NOTES

◉ Have you ever tried to do something good but experienced so much tension that it seemed like "God wasn't in it?" As you look back now, how would you change the way you viewed that opposition? Has your opinion changed?

◉ Why do you think we tend to choose a path without tension? How does that impact our ability to experience new things of faith? How does it threaten your desire to continue or even increase your commitment to serve?

◉ One of the tensions you're going to experience as a group is wrestling with how to continue engaging need. What role do you think you should play in making sure you continue to grow together?

◉ What is your greatest fear moving forward? What has been your favorite part? Write them below, then offer them both to God as a prayer.

THE INTUITIVE LIFE_*reCreate*

**Consider this:** There is a strong connection between a regular rhythm of rest and the ability to clearly hear the Spirit and live an intuitive life. This is what makes it possible for us to "never tire of doing what is good." A mind and heart set on earthly things and human effort finds little peace. We not only get our direction and strength from the Holy Spirit, but we find our rest, for his glory, in him as well.

## CLOSING

# What's next?

My wife and I recently adopted two beautiful children from Ethiopia, a 5-year-old girl and a 7-year-old boy. As I write this, we're deep in the throes of parenting children who've seen and experienced things no one should have to endure. We're building hope, gaining trust, redefining family, and leaning heavily on our faith and our faith community.

Adoption has been the greatest struggle, yet the most rewarding journey, of my life. Amidst it all, there have been some incredibly joyful moments.

One of my favorites was standing in Walmart with my little girl as she picked out her first bike. Although it was a bit small for her, she chose the pink one, which didn't surprise any of us. Thankfully, it was the one with training wheels.

She had no idea how to navigate a bicycle. So the training wheels were necessary. Keeping the handlebars straight while actually turning the pedals proved to be quite a difficult task for her. Turning the corner without tipping over was another. Riding a bike was something I could talk about and even show her, but it was something she had to experience herself in order to really learn. As expected, she eventually figured it out and began to experience first hand how fun a bike can be.

Last week, I took off the training wheels. While at first it felt like we were starting over, we weren't. She had safely learned the basics that she could now apply to help her realize the full potential of her bike. Today, I'm taking her to buy a bigger bike that fits her. While she loves her little pink beginner bike, I know she'll love her new one even more.

The *Barefoot Church Primer* is like training wheels to help you learn to serve through community. And now it's time to take them off. We can't just continue riding with them, keeping only to the basics, and expect the adventure to continue.

For some of you, this journey may have seemed elementary. For others, deeply revealing. Our prayer is that somehow you've gained some insight into foundational truths that are critical for social action to become and remain Gospel-centered, redemptive, transformational, as well as community building.

As you know, this journey is not over. In fact, it's only just begun. We can't allow service to remain a program or monthly routine. Somehow we need to make it more personal. We need to be praying that, as we serve, we will be transformed and that a heart for the broken will be cultivated. Somehow we must invest ourselves beyond the surface. It has to change us, those we serve with, and those we serve.

Our hope is that you continue to navigate what this looks like. Don't give up on each other. As you wrestle with what you've been doing, be in prayer, be in conversation, and keep going. Consider what opportunities exist to invest relationally in making a longer term difference. Keep educating yourselves on needs you can engage with as a part of the natural rhythm of your life. Consider ways to become good news. Think about how to involve others who might be resistant to "church-as-usual." Continue to build and maintain a holistic view of service.

As you do so, our hope is that the Spirit will lead you beyond whatever is in your immediate path, and will give you a longing to make an even greater difference in the world. We pray that you see the orphan crisis and feel their pain. That you see poverty and injustice and you feel indignation. That you hear about human trafficking and can no longer sit in silence. God doesn't need us to fix this world. Yet he's invited us into his plan of restoration. Scripture challenges us to learn, to focus on our daily journey, and to trust the Gospel. We pray that as you do, you will find even more of Jesus, the one who literally poured out his life for you and me.

*"Let your light shine before others, that they may see your good deeds and glorify your Father in heaven."* - Jesus

# Resources by Missio and Missio Publishing

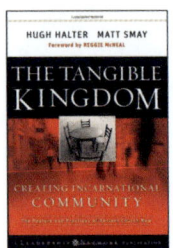 

The story of *Missio* is described in detail in ***The Tangible Kingdom: Creating Incarnational Community*** by Hugh Halter and Matt Smay. The book has a companion guide called the ***Tangible Kingdom Primer*** which is designed to help Christians, churches, and small groups get on the pathway of spiritual formation and missional engagement. The primer creates opportunities to experience authentic missional community. It leads participants on a challenging 8-week journey toward an incarnational lifestyle and moves far beyond the typical small group experience.

 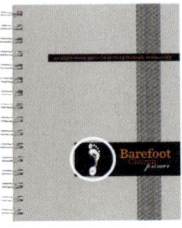

Brandon Hatmaker's book ***Barefoot Church*** and the corresponding resource the ***Barefoot Church Primer*** tell the next chapter in the *Missio* story. The *Barefoot Church Primer* provides practical steps toward living out the Good News of Jesus in a world full of need. The primer creates a unique opportunity to invite Christians from all backgrounds as well as non-Christian friends to join you in serving the least. The 8-week study works to naturally create a wealth of missional ministry openings as an outcome of learning to serve the least together.

In addition to these two books and the two corresponding primers, *Missio* develops training and resources to help your church take a more systematic approach to engaging in community and mission. The book **AND: The Gathered and Scattered Church** is written to help pastors guide churches into a more balanced and more missional mindset. The *Missio* website has many other resources, with more on the way, to help leaders cast vision and begin recruiting people to pilot incarnational communities. VIsit **www.missio.us** for more information about our training and other resources.

Missio Publishing is committed to resourcing the church with practical tools to help it engage more effectively in missional and incarnational ministry. To purchase the Primers and other resources, along with bulk discounts for churches, visit **www.missiopublishing.com**